BOOK TO SCREEN

How to Adapt Your Novel

Into a Screenplay

FRANK CATALANO

BOOK TO SCREEN
HOW TO ADAPT YOUR NOVEL INTO A SCREENPLAY

COMPILATION OF SEMINARS HELD AT THE 25TH ANNUAL WRITER'S CONFERENCE
SAN DIEGO STATE UNIVERSITY

Copyright © 2009 / 2015 Frank Catalano
All rights reserved. No part of this book may be reproduced or transmitted in any form or by any means without written permission from the author.
ISBN-13: 9780692282946
ISBN-10: 0692282947
Lexington Avenue Press
www.lexingtonavepress.com
818-994-2779

Books by Frank Catalano

Art of the Monologue
Monologues they haven't heard yet

The Creative Audience
*The collaborative role of the audience
In the creation of the visual and performing arts*

White Knight Black Night
Short monologues for auditions

The Resting Place
a play

Autumn Sweet
a play

Rand Unwrapped
Confessions of a Robotech Warrior

Che Che
A screenplay

Short Monologues for Auditions

Book to Screen is a compilation of lectures presented by Frank Catalano as part of the 25th Annual Writer's Conference. The conference was sponsored by San Diego State University on February 6 through the 8th, 2009 at the Double Tree Hilton Hotel in Mission Hills, California. The following transcripts were presented and recorded by Frank Catalano as part of the programs offered at the conference. This book is in part based upon this and other seminars presented by Mr. Catalano.

Writers of fiction and non-fiction and industry professionals from the publishing business primarily attended the 25th Annual Writer's Conference. Mr. Catalano's seminars focused upon those writers seeking to adapt their novels into screenplays. The complete list of seminar presentations by Frank Catalano for this conference that have been published as individual volumes are:

Book 1: *Writing Great Characters in the First Ten Pages*
Book 2: *Writing on Your Feet– IMPROVISATIONAL TECHNIQUES FOR WRITERs – Part 1*
Book 3: *Start Your Story at the End*
Book 4: *The First Ten Pages*
Book 5: *Book to Screen* (compiled volume – Books 1 - 7)
Book 6 *Acting It Out – IMPROVISATIOINAL TECHNIQUES FOR WRITERS - Part 2*
Book 7 *Writing Great Dialogue*

TABLE OF CONTENTS

Introduction   xiii

Book 1:   *Writing Great Charatcters in the First Ten Pages*   1

1. Page to Screen   3
2. What an Audience Expects of You   7
3. Your Pitch   13
4. Getting Your Adapted Screenplay Read   19
5. Always Put Yourself in the Audience   23
6. Adaptation – Your First Ten Script Pages   33
7. Wrapping It Up   41

Book 2:   *Writing On Your Feet*
Improvisational Techniques for Writers – Part 1   43

8. Writing on Your Feet   45
9. Writing Using Moving Pictures   49
10. Writing Using Your Five Senses   55
11. Manipulation versus Selection   61
12. Writing Using Improvisation   63
13. You Don't Have To Be Funny to Improvise   71
14. Finding the Metaphor – How ***Not*** to be Literal   81

Book 3:	***Start Your Story at the End***	**91**

15. What I Learned Working at a Motion Picture Studio — 93
16. Adapting your Novel into a Screenplay — 97
17. Write Like You're Buying Toothpaste — 101
18. Presenting Your Story to an Audience — 105
19. Everyone is concerned with the end result not the process — 109
20. Visualize Your Book as a Movie Trailer — 113
21. Rosebud — 121
22. Write Like a Painter — 129
23. Who is Your Target Audience? — 139
24. Start Your Story at the End — 143

Book 4:	***The First Ten Pages***	**147**

25. Location Location Location — 149
26. Creating Inevitability in the First Ten Pages — 153
27. Let's Go to the Movies — 159
28. Instant Gratification — 167
29. Write Like You're a Pole Dancer in a Strip Club — 175
30. The Road Not Taken — 181
31. Your First Ten Pages Description, Action and Dialogue — 185
32. A Rose By Any Other Name Having the Right Title — 193
33. Begin at the End — 197

Book 5:	***Book to Screen***	**201**

34. Rejection — 203
35. Know Where You Are Going – Identify your Market — 207
36. Working Your Way to ***Yes*** — 213

Book 6: *Acting it out*
Improvisational Techniques for Writers – Part 2 **219**

37. Using Improvisation to Develop Your Characters
 and Story 221
38. Improvisation as a Creative Journey 231
39. Improvisation as a Creative Tool 237
40. Using Physicality to Create Characters and Tell
 Your Story 241
41. Page to Screen - Description Action and Dialogue 247
42. Let Your Characters Experience Your Story
 Through Their Five Senses 255
43. Developing Character - The Three "P's" 259
44. How Bouncing a Ball Can Become Flying a Kite 265
45. Acting it out 269

Book 7: *Writing Great Dialogue* **271**

46. Writing Great Dialogue 273
47. Production Distribution Exhibition 275
48. Description Action Dialogue 279
49. What Does Dialogue Do? 283
50. Other Qualities of Dialogue 293

BOOK TO SCREEN

How to Adapt Your Novel Into a Screenplay

COMPILATION OF SEMINARS HELD AT THE 25TH ANNUAL WRITER'S CONFERENCE SAN DIEGO STATE UNIVERSITY

FRANK CATALANO

INTRODUCTION

I WANT TO welcome you to BOOK TO SCREEN and the 25th Annual Writer's Conference. It has been a great weekend!

Okay, we are a very eclectic group today from all parts of the country so this is going to be a lot of fun. What I want to talk to all of you about today is the conversion of a novel to a screenplay. There are several different ways I want to approach this topic. But first, for those of you that I haven't already met, I wanted to provide to you a little bit of background information about me. Before I forget, I am also sending around a sheet so that you can put your name and an email address so that I can send you written notes from today's presentation. That is of course optional – you do not have to provide contact information.

My name is Frank Catalano. I am a college professor teaching at the School of Theatre (now School of Dramatic Arts as of 2012). I teach acting, writing and theatre and all different kinds of elements of presentational performance. I also teach Humanities courses that include visual and performing arts: painting, sculpture, film, television and audience studies. My acting classes are both on camera and stage. As a theatre producer/playwright I have had productions at the Beverly Hills Playhouse in Los Angeles and have had shows produced in New York City and other parts of the country.

In addition to academia, I was an executive at Warner Brothers Studios and Lorimar Productions probably the longest. I had various positions including consultancies, packaging, marketing and writing. I had what is called a **first look writing agreement** at Warner Brothers for the development of motion pictures and television productions. Working at a movie studio is a great experience. The studio provides a framework to develop everything you write although they are not obligated to produce it. So you set up shop there, you write, you work with other writers sometimes. But, the hard part of that process is that not very much gets actually made. In a large studio universe, producing was something totally different than writing. I just primarily focused on the writing.

I am also an author. *I have two books out: *Art of the Monologue (2007)*. It's a theatre book for actors with original monologues and a large section on monologue performance theory. I've also had plays produced and published. I have a new play being published right now and I have a brand new book coming out this month called *The Creative Audience – The Collaborative Role of the Audience in the Creation of Visual and Performing Arts (2009)* and so it is not being sold in the lobby.

*Since this 2009 presentation, Frank Catalano has published the following books:

> *Art of the Moologue (2007)*
> *The Creative Audience (2009)*
> *White Knight Black Night – Short Monologues for Auditions (2010)*
> *Autumn Sweet – a Play (2011)*
> *The Resting Place – a Play (2011)*
> *Rand Unwrapped – Confessions of a Robotech Warrior (2013)*
> *Che Che – A Screenplay (2013)*
> *Short Monologues for Auditions (2013)*

Today, in this final presentation I want to put together all of the seminars we have had this weekend. So some of this is review and there will also be some new material.

So, let's get started.

WRITING GREAT CHARATCTERS IN THE FIRST TEN PAGES

SAN DIEGO STATE UNIVERSITY
25th Annual Writers Conference

WORKSHOP TRANSCRIPT
HOW TO ADAPT YOUR NOVEL INTO A SCREENPLAY

BOOK 1

Frank Catalano

1

PAGE TO SCREEN

Writing Great Characters in the First Ten Pages

THE PRESENTATION OF your work to others is almost as important as the idea (the work) itself. That's what I was thinking of before I came here today to meet all of you. What would be the best "frame" to put this seminar in? WRITING GREAT CHARACTERS IN THE FIRST TEN PAGES? What does this title actually mean? Let's think of it this way. We have all probably been to McDonalds or Burger King?

    (Audience laughter)

I know you have. You probably won't admit it.

    (Audience laughter)

And what are you getting? We "hope" that it's a beef patty. Right? And why did we go there? Because eating fast good is a fast and inexpensive way to eat. We didn't go there for the atmosphere. Now let's take that same beef patty and place it in a really fancy restaurant. In Los Angles, we have Wolfgang Puck's Grill in Beverly Hills. Now let's take that same hamburger patty and maybe change the shape of it a little so it doesn't look like a patty. We add carrots, potatoes, garnish sauce and other things around it. Present it in soft amber lighting, candles, and violin music playing... and now that hamburger patty that was under a dollar costs thirty dollars.

(Audience laughter)

But what has changed? Nothing. The only thing that's changed is the frame that the "patty" has been placed within. And this is important to stress. It is not a lie in the sense that I'm not taking out the patty and putting it in my pocket and replacing it with a filet mignon steak. No, it's the same patty. What **has** changed is the point of view and the framework of the presentation. That is the most important thing. The idea remains the same. By extension, the process for writing characters or converting characters from a novel is quite the same thing. It's all how you frame them at the start of your story.

I want to explore the differences between the two mediums. So with that in mind, how many of you are active screenwriters?

(Audience member raising hand)

I've got one... I've got two. And you?

(Audience member: "Off and on...")

But you have written screenplays. Have any of your screenplays been put into production?

(Audience member: "No, but it's been work shopped.")

Okay. How about you?

(Audience member: "I'm going to make my own film.")

Great! Wonderful. And you know what? That's the future. When you go to Warner Brothers and other majors and they might tell you, "Well, we just don't know what to do with your project... it doesn't fit in... it just won't work for us." Then there people, right out of film school, that don't know the rules (that's a good thing). They aren't aware of what they are supposed to do or not do because the schools they attend never prepare them that way.

(Audience laughter)

They go out and they create a short film, a trailer or series of webisodes on YouTube and now they have something tangible to show the world. The discussion can be quite different then. "I have four films up on YouTube or Vimeo and have 50,000 or 100,000 hits. Would you like to view it?" What are they actually looking at? Yes, a sample of the writer's work. But they are looking at much more. The work they view is a movie or series that would probably have never been made. So this is a very good way to go if you are developing your novel into a screenplay. You can do the same thing. You can put up portions of your work (trailers). When I say post, I mean shoot scenes or readings and put them up.

So, what do I want to say about writing great characters in the first ten pages? It's a catchy title. I'm going to be straight with you.

(Audience laughter)

It really should be *WRITNG GREAT CHARACTERS FOR THE MEDIUM* or *WRITING GREAT CHARACTERS FOR A PRESENTATION*. But then, you wouldn't come. But you are saying "What about the first ten pages?" Let's talk about that. Writing great characters, we all want to do that. That's a given... and we are primarily fiction writers (novels) and you have your characters set up in your books and within that medium, you have a certain methodology of development and narrative. You have the ability to to stop in the middle of a story and go into the childhood or a past event, which tells the reader something significant about your character. However, in film (and I will break down film into television and film) you don't have that luxury. There is a general framework in feature film writing of approximately how long the screenplay should be and then on the production side how long the final film should be in relationship to the audience expectation. How long is an audience willing to sit in a darkened theatre watching a particular film? Probably, two hours for a normal showing of a story and maybe longer say three hours for a larger subject like *Gandhi (1982), Dances with Wolves (1990)* or *Titanic (1997)*. There is an expectation of run time here. In film, you can't meander off the main narrative for very long or risk losing your script reader or audience.

2

What an Audience Expects of You

Writing Great Characters in the First Ten Pages

We're all an audience at some time or another. When you go to the movies and we all go, what would you think if I were to say to you – ask you – what is the appropriate run time for a motion picture? In other words, if you get all dressed up, walk out the door and you buy your ticket for an 8:00 PM showing and you attend the whole showing, when do you expect to return home? Assuming you don't stop somewhere after the movie.

(Audience response – two hours… about ten o'clock.)

Yes, ten o'clock. And what if you're going to the opera?

(Audience laughter)

Nobody here goes to the opera? Are you with me on that one?

(Audience laughter)

I went to the opera CARMEN at the Dorothy Chandler Pavilion (home of the Los Angeles Opera) with Placido Domingo conducting and I sat there with my daughter. After Act 1, Act 2, there was a short intermission and I said to her, "Honey that was great!" I thought it was over because two and half hours had passed. She smiled at me and said; "Dad, it's just the intermission."

(Audience laughter)

"There are another three acts." Three acts? So, I went straight to the bar.

(Audience laughter)

Okay, anyway… so there is a certain audience expectation, which is somehow attached to the medium in which a work of art (film, television show, novel) is presented. No one wrote this down. There are no traffic cops there if it is not followed. But there is an unstated expectation. Certain media or mediums evoke a specific audience expectation. There is some evidence typically in motion pictures that this is the case.

If we were to go back in time to let's say 1939 when 90 million people went to the movies every week. When you attended a movie in 1939, you looked up at the theatre marquee and it might have had a particular actor's name above the title. Something like "Judy Garland in the MGM Sensation – THE WIZARD OF OZ." But above it all would be the name of the studio that owned the theatre – Paramount, Warner's, MGM/Lowe's, Fox or Universal. These were the five major studios at the time. My point is the production entity which might have been Paramount or Warners – any one of the big five owned the production of that film, hired (as contract employees) all the above the line (as non contract employees) and below the line creative people. They also owned one hundred percent of the distribution and owned the physical theatre – the brick and mortar building where the film was exhibited.

(New female audience member enters the room – but there are no seats. Catalano, provides his own.)

Here take mine. Chivalry is not dead.

(Audience laughter)

Why don't you sit right over here?

And they owned the physical theatres (brick and mortar), which meant... if the movie (run time) ran long, they didn't care. If the movie was bad, they didn't care.

(Audience laughter)

...of course they want the films to be good. But really, it didn't matter because they knew they had 90 million plus people a week going to the movies. No matter what.

(Audience laughter)

No, seriously... and it was given. They could put a chicken chasing a worm up on the screen and they knew they were going to make their numbers. Why? They owned the very seats the audience sat on. They owned the candy, the popcorn. They owned everything and were able to keep all of the money they made after costs. What about today?

Today, let's use the same example. Paramount is part of a larger corporation – Viacom that owns the studio, may own the distribution of a particular film. However, they no longer own the physical movie theatres. Studios had to give up ownership of exhibition (movie theatres) in 1948 by order of the Supreme Court (Paramount Decree). Movie theatres today are owned by exhibition entities independent of the producing company of a particular film. What this means is that all those multiplexes we go to are separate corporate chains that Paramount (Viacom) has to negotiate with to place a film for exhibition.

Because of this, there is always an indelible pressure on the major studios (production) to make films that exhibitors want to show and an audience wants to see. In many cases that means shorter films and shorter movie trailers with less spoilers. It has nothing to do with our (audience) expectation as much as it has to do with the profit motives of exhibitors. Exhibitors want to fill as many seats as possible (within a given time frame). So, if they have "Theatre A" and it has 300 seats, they want to be able to have the maximum number of showing in that space in a given day. If you have a longer run time, longer trailers, it is going to prevent that from happening. Long running films like *Titanic (1997) The Ring (2002) or Dances with Wolves(1990)* will cut down on the number of times a given space can provide showings in a given day. Of course, movie exhibitors can counter this by offering the same film in a number of spaces within their theatre at one time.

(Audience member calls out: "*Pearl Harbor.*")

Pearl Harbor. That's right. Run time over three hours.

(Audience member: "Also, they are running more ad time.")

I'm not even counting that in the run time

(Audience laughter)

I'm just talking about what we write. You bring up an interesting point because one of the other considerations is product placement within the creative work. This off topic but is defined as the seamless integration of advertising and products into content. I've was at a meeting once it was actually discussed that the script itself was not the best but that it should be considered because of its product placement and merchandising potential. They felt they could figure out a way to make it better and that's another story. But product placement can work within a certain degree. I'm thinking of the film Tom Hank's did when he was stranded on the island after the plane crash.

(Audience member: "*Cast Away.*")

Right– the motion picture – *Castaway* (2000). Does anyone remember the role that FEDEX played in that film? The whole story was framed around a FedEx plane crashing and at the end Tom Hanks delivers a FedEx package that had been with him on the island. Don't know if you remember, the girl looked single and was very pretty. How can you beat that for feel good advertising – FedEx always comes through (no matter what) and maybe a loving relationship there as well. Can't beat that.

I think a film where product placement is not so seamless would be *Iron Man* (2008) where the cars, pizzas, hamburgers were all too present in the way they were placed within the film.

(Audience laughter)

So there is an indelible pressure in cinema for the final product to be … I'm not going to say fixed, but rather a general understanding of runtime for a particular film. This is not present in literature.

So let me ask… are most of your books 300 pages? 250 pages? About 60,000 to 70, 000 words. Anyone over that? Okay, that's right, you already told me that. Anyone over 400 pages… 100,000 words?

(Audience member raises hand)

I'm not saying that is bad. I love those books painted upon a broad canvass. I mean when you read a good book like that, you can settle in and go with it. You know you are going to be with it for a while… which is great. So all of you, the "plus 300 crowd," I'm speaking to you.

Now you've taken this beautifully written manuscript with character development and everything we are talking about and now you have to squeeze all of it into a little square hole that runs on the average 120 pages of dialogue, description and action. So, there is a challenge there. You have to make choices about how to convert what is contained in the longer literary medium where the spoken word and language are used into a visual medium and context for film. You have to consider different methods to make this happen. Earlier this week we discussed starting your screenplay at the most heightened moment of your novel or as it was titled BEGINNING YOUR SCREENPLAY AT THE END. How would you do this? Short answer. You can accomplish this by showing your story through visual exposition. But that's a different seminar. Let's get back to our subject... Writing great characters (we are back on the title). We all want to write great characters. We all want to write great stories.

Now for the second part of our seminar title "IN THE FIRST TEN PAGES." What's that's mean? It's something you put in the title. But there's a little bit of truth to it. Okay, and here it is. We live in a society and I'm not saying anything you don't already know. It's an "immediate gratification" society where we have come to expect everything "now" through, televisions, portable hand held devices and the cloud. We don't want to go through anything that might take too much time. We want it **now**. We don't want a *"slow roll"* or too much process in getting to what we came for. It's the same in story telling. You have to get to it as soon as possible or risk losing your audience.

Although you could probably this afternoon list a multitude of very successful movies that have what I am calling a "slow roll." You know you just kind of pull into them nice and easy through a process of character development and exposition. I'm thinking of films like *Forrest Gump (1994)* or *2001 A Space Odyssey (1968)* where you're sitting in the theatre wondering where the story is going. But for our purposes here today, I want you to think about creating the most important elements (including characters) of your script right away... and if you can, in the first ten pages.

3

YOUR PITCH

Writing Great Characters in the First Ten Pages

Now let's go a step further if we could. I'm sure some of you went to some of the pitch
workshops here. And now take your wonderful book and try to pitch your entire idea and manuscript in three or four sentences. They listen and then they tell you "We are interested in your book – we would like to develop it into a screenplay. Do you have a screenplay?" And you answer: "Yes, I have a screenplay." They set up a pitch meeting. Next you find yourself sitting at Warner Brothers or Paramount and someone sitting across a desk or on a couch says "Alright, give me your story." And they are talking about that they want your story in a format of no longer than a minute. Now we are going from one mode of presentation to another. We are going from the "full meal" which is your manuscript/book in its entirety, into the shorter version of the screenplay and then even the more abbreviated form of the pitch. This screenplay is not even in consideration. We are simply talking about and idea. I've heard writers say that they have written a really phenomenal screenplay but they never get the actual script in front of anyone because it missed the pitch. What I mean by that is, the have forgotten

the idea and got pulled into mechanical process of writing. Don't forget the idea. It sounds very Zen but it's true. Don't get kidnapped by the screenplay or the novel. Always go back to the idea and the pitch. Let everything emanate from that and be ready to have something in your back pocket at a moments notice. That is "if" they don't like your idea, be ready to pitch them something else.

I will tell you a funny story about a pitch. Well, it's not that funny.

(Audience laughter)

There was this one writer, kind of a nerdy guy, but very smart and very nice. He underwent a process of research and study of the Apollo moon landings. He researched NASA transcripts of all of the Apollo missions to the moon. Project Apollo was America's effort to land a man on the moon and bring him back before the end of the nineteen sixties. This was a challenge set forth by former President John Kennedy and began what was known in the 1960's as the moon race. It was a competition between the United States and the former Soviet Union to land a man on the moon first. The decade was filled with an array of space missions by both countries focusing on getting there first. In the Cold War era, whomever could land a man on the moon first, would have the upper hand in the propaganda war between the two countries and their respective political ideologies. So, it was very important for each country to get there first, no matter what. In July of 1969, the question was answered when America's Neal Armstrong was the first man to walk on the moon on national television. It was a great achievement for mankind and an even greater propaganda victory for the United States over the Soviet Union.

Now, getting back to the writer and his pitch. He developed a theory that history had got it all wrong and that the Russians had actually landed on the moon first and nobody knew about it because it was covered up. And it was not just idle speculation. This writer had specific transcripts of astronauts communicating with mission control.

(Garbled sound effect)

"Houston we've got a problem." I don't think they actually said that but I'm just trying to act it out for you.

(Audience laughter)

His pitch was to tell a story that would radically change history, as we knew it. His story would be told on a larger than life canvass -- outer space and would be filled with intrigue and mystery. In the late, 1960's a spacecraft is launched from Russia on a journey to the moon and then is never heard of or mentioned again. It was a failed mission and no one not even the Russians knew what happened to the spacecraft. What they could not have known was that the spacecraft landed a man on the moon (a Russian cosmonaut) first – before the United States. A single cosmonaut had crash- landed but had lost the ability to communicate with the Soviet space agency on earth. The Soviet space agency assumed the spacecraft trajectory had missed the moon and was lost in space. They had no way of knowing that the cosmonaut successfully landed on the moon and (after his supplies and oxygen ran out) died there. America went on to take the trophy in the moon race. The fate of the cosmonaut was never known until several years later when NASA astronauts discovered the Soviet craft as they were exploring the lunar surface. The U.S. policy was to keep the discovery a secret to avoid the embarrassment of erasing such an American achievement. Besides the Russians didn't even know it occurred, so why rock the boat?

A Pretty compelling concept and there was also a backstory that spanned to the end of World War II. So, (this writer) he's ready with his story and has facts to back it up – all lined up. I mean this guy is pumped.

(Pump sounds – Audience laughter.)

He arrives at the meeting and he has what I thought was an okay script. It was a good script but not a great script. It didn't have any heat. It had intellect but no heat. You know when somebody tells you an idea about such a conspiracy, that they say they can prove, creates interest. I'm interested and wondered if it really happened. The script needed some work but that was not the problem because the script never got read. At the meeting, the producer (no name) asked, "Okay, what'ya got for me?" It wasn't a guy with a cigar in his mouth but it felt that way.

(Audience laughter)

"All right, kid…what'ya got?"

Remember, the entire storyline and concept had to be boiled down into one simple idea. The writer looked the producer and said: "All right, here it is. The Russians landed on the moon first… and nobody knows about it."

The producer responded after a moment: "Who gives a crap. Nobody cares about that. What else you got?"

(Audience sighs)

It was that fast. That was it. Nobody cares about that. Period. And so I said to myself. That pitch, what was lacking in the pitch? Let's blame the writer not the producer because the presentation didn't have the spirit of the original idea. It didn't have it. The writer had cut it down so much, that there was no soul left in it. He was no longer offering him a representation of the full idea – instead a small component of it with no connection to the whole and because of that, it ceased to be interesting. I don't know? I have endeavored to think about what he could have said that would have been more interesting. It's easy for me to stand here today and criticize. But the writer never got the chance to have the script read. Not at that studio anyway and point of it was that what failed there was not the idea. It was the mode of presentation.

With respect to mode of presentation, always ask yourself these questions:

1. What environment/situation am I presenting this idea in?
2. How can I make my idea fit that environment/situation?

Is it a Burger King hamburger or is it Wolfgang Puck? In the instance of this moon story pitch, the environment and the presentation were not in sync. The producer was expecting something else. How can you make the idea fit the mode? This is an art into itself. If the producer is looking for the writer to give him a one-line concept presentation – perhaps the writer should make his line a question?

A larger question. Something like this.

Writer: What if I told you something that nobody knows about?

Producer: There's very little I don't know about.

Writer: Okay, who landed on the moon?

Producer: The moon, we landed on the moon? I'm only kidding… the Americans did… everybody knows that. Tell me something I don't know.

Writer: You're wrong… the Russians did and the American's lied about it.

Producer: Really…

Writer: …and if they lied about that, what else don't you know?

Maybe that would be enough to peek the interest of the producer to get coverage on the script. Then again, maybe not. At least, the writer in my scenario tried to pull the producer in and then at least get a read. When you pitch you have got to create the mode of presentation that best fits the situation. You select the mode of presentation. Take control of the room. It's your moment and you decide how it's going to be played out – good or bad. That's the pitch.

Now, on to the next mode of presentation – getting your adapted script read.

4

GETTING YOUR ADAPTED SCREENPLAY READ

Writing Great Characters in the First Ten Pages

THE NEXT MODE of presentation would be the reading of your script. You now are getting an initial "read." Producer A, B or C says that they would love to read your script. That's what they will tell you but do you actually believe they will read it? No, the script will be given to a reader for coverage and you hope they see what you see in the story. So now your life and your creation is now being entrusted to someone you haven't even met. You might not even know the producer. But now it's being entrusted to someone else – a third party. And they analyze it on a level that may not have anything to do with your creative idea. It (your idea) will be considered for budget. How many of you are doing period pieces?

(Audience – several hands are raised)

Okay, you can imagine the problem with period, is that it costs more money. You may write a brilliant script but it may get shot down simply because the company where you have submitted it may no want to do period pieces or high budgets. So you look at it and you say

"Okay, I'm now presenting my work in a third person mode – in which that third person, I don't know, is going to read and evaluate it." That's where the ten pages come in!

You have got to present the most compelling elements of your characters and story up front. Because they may only read part of it and then turn to the end of your script to see how many pages it is. Now, what does that mean? It means nothing or it means everything. If you write a script (in the proper format) for a feature length film and it's 120 – 130 pages, you're okay. If it's 190, you've got a problem… Houston.

(Audience laughter)

Because they are judging you already and they know all the tricks a writer can use to make a longer script appear to be shorter. Smaller fonts, they know all that. You use standard font and hand them a 150-180 page script, it's already got one strike against it. It communicates to the reader/producer that you are not familiar with the intended medium. That's all it means. Then next thing they do is they look at your script and in those first ten pages they are making assumptions about the entire work. If the characters and story contained within the first ten pages are compelling then reason would dictate that the rest of the script is that way as well. It's like when two people meet in a bar or restaurant, one asks, "Hey what do you do?" and the other says, "I dig ditches." Then the first makes the assumption "Not interesting… I'll move on to someone else."

(Audience laughter)

Reading a script is similar to when two people meet for the first time – they are investing in the first ten minutes (pages)… and within those ten minutes they make a decision about the other person – whether they want to know more about them or not. In the case of your script, they do the same thing—they make assumptions right from the start and decide whether or not to go further. And that's the way people are. It has nothing to do about being good or bad – they are all in hurry to have an answer. That's what they are paid to do. Have an answer. It doesn't mean, that they won't absolutely read the rest of your script if they don't like the beginning. They probably will and do. But you want to be at least at "zero" in the beginning. Zero is that absolute place where it all begins with no prejudice at all upon what you have written. But you don't want to be a t below zero – that's having someone reading your script feeling that it is a chore and that they would rather be doing something else. You want to be at least at zero or better when they start off believing your work has possibilities. This is good. This is good. You want them to keep reading and stead of saying to themselves (this sucks) and then skimming the rest to the end. If your best material is on page fifty-five –they may never truly get there. When that happens, you have lost.

I'm into simplicity. But I want the best (most compelling) parts first. Yesterday, we did an entire hour about starting your screenplay at the end. That was about starting your story at the most intense moment and then filling in the details through exposition. It's a heightened sense of reality. Isn't that what Alfred Hitchcock once said: "Drama is life… with the dull parts cut out." The same applies to the development of your characters. Get to their high point right away – put a mongoose and a cobra face to face right at the start and then show us what can happen. Then give them the rest of the story as you go. Then at least the audience is with you; they are at the party, on the bus, on the train. Whatever analogy you want to use. And they will take the journey with you. Now remember, just because you have written compelling characters doesn't mean it's a sure thing.

Now your script may not make the cut for reasons beyond your control. Reasons that have nothing to do with the quality of your writing including they may not have the budget, the may be looking for a certain type of project (that yours is not) or they may have a specific cast in mind that it doesn't fit. You can't control all the variables but at least you got the read and you can "live to fight / write another day." You will have more manuscripts and next time (now that you have a relationship) you will have something they want. I also, am a believer that the universe will provide. Sometimes you really want something to happen and when it doesn't you become discouraged only to learn that something even better awaits you just around the corner.

(Audience laughter)

My point here is to front load your work as much as you can to compel or propel your reader (whatever term you like) to consider your work and give it their fullest attention.

That's why we say WRITING GREAT CHARACTERS IN THE FIRST TEN PAGES.

In all honesty, no one is counting if you introduce the strongest most compelling elements of character fully by eleven or twelve pages. It's okay. The importance is that it is at the front. Now let's get to one more mode of presentation. You're sitting in the theatre and your book or screenplay has been made into a movie. See it, you're sitting in a darkened theatre as the credits roll... everyone is going to say here... yeah I wish.

(Audience laughter)

5

Always Put Yourself in the Audience

Writing Great Characters in the First Ten Pages

A COUPLE OF THINGS had to happen. Somewhere along the line, your 250-300 page novel was squeezed into a screenplay. Either you wrote the script or someone else did. So, choices had to be made. What to include what to leave out, then the shooting script was interpreted by a director, later an editor and star. Your original work may have been changed dramatically to fit into the movie you are about to watch. And you are thinking, "My name is on it… what if it's terrible?" The creation of film is a collaborative art and you hope you have a good director, editor and actors. But assuming they are all very talented and you are there (in the theatre) and after the opening credits – the story begins. The same rule applies, within the first ten minutes of the film; the audience needs to be connected to the main characters and story.

In the first two minutes of *(Jurassic Park 1993)* the audience sees and hears the menacing Velociraptor as it's cage is brought in by a forklift. We don't actually see the whole dinosaur, we just see it's eye and that's really all we need. We're hooked and have to stay to find out what is going to happen.

All this in happens in less than ten minutes. I'm using the number 10 again. Within the first ten minutes of the exhibition of the movie the audience should have an idea of who the main characters are and they should know something about them. And if they don't, there's a problem. Now the Velociraptor is certainly not the main character for this story, but it is a pivotal force within the story and frames the main characters the audience meets shortly after this scene. This is essential character development and story telling.

How many times have you been to the movies or a play and you are watching it but you really don't know who the characters are or what it's about? Has anyone ever been there?

(Audience reaction – "Yes")

And then there are examples when an audience can know too much – and they are board seeing what they already know played out over and over again. And then there's the Goldilocks scenario – when it's all just right. Not too little, not too much… just right. That's where you want to be.

Have any of you seen the movie *Doubt (2008)?* All right, it was a good movie and within the first three setups of the film – the sermon scene delivered by the late Philip Seymour Hoffman – about two or three minutes into the film, we are introduced to Sister Aloysius played by Meryl Streep. As the sermon is given, she walks quietly down the aisle (we haven't seen her face yet) behind a young boy who is horsing around and slaps him in the back of the head. She then continues walking silently down the isle (as the sermon continues) and comes upon a young boy leaning forward in the pew with his head buried into his arms – he is sleeping. It is here that we finally get our first glimpse of Sister Aloysius's face when she snaps at the lad and whispers "Straighten it!" The boy jumps back to his seat in attention. After that moment, she stands straight and upright and we get a full view of her face. In a few short moments, the audience has been connected to this character and we can imagine that a lot of the pull comes from Streep's performance – but she is working as an actor creating a character within the framework of the writer.

When I say the audience has to know about your character in the first ten pages, I'm not saying they have to know their social security number or anything like that. They have to know the important aspects of your character – so much so that they want to learn more and make the journey.

What about *The Wrestler (2008)*? Has anyone here seen this film?

(Audience – no replies)

You guys have got to get out more.

(Audience laughter)

It opens with the lead character doing what he does. He's in the ring fighting. It is the same idea as the motion picture DOUBT. You are pulled in to his world and you know right off the bat what's going on with this guy. You might say to yourself: "I have never been a wrestler, so what do I know about that? How can I identify with that?" Right? But you may think about it another way. "But I do know something about being on the ropes or knowing people that have been on the ropes who want to pull themselves out of whatever they are in." We all want change? Change for the better? Don't we? I think so. We all want to make our lives better. So this guy happens to be a wrestler who is fighting for a second chance at his life. We can all understand the desire to change because we want to change. And so, we're on the bus – we've paid our money to take the journey.

(Audience – reaction – agreement)

Let's think about one other example that's new. Any of you see the new film out called *The Reader (2008)*?

(Audience laughter because no one has seen it)

Really, we should just go to the movies tonight.

(Audience laughter)

Here's the deal. THE READER starts off – I'm not going to tell you the whole story but I will tell you a little. I have a problem with THE READER and will tell you that much. My problem is not so much the film as the way it has been marketed as a Nazi movie. And it is about Nazi's in a very abstract way. It's not a movie in anyway about Nazi's – our favorite villains.

(Audience laughter)

Nazi's are such great bad boys you just love to hate. However, the Nazi element of the film is only an instrument to further the characters. It is not a major part of the plot. It's not about the reader (Kate Winslet) being a Nazi prison guard at all. It is really about how two people come together (I've already said too much) and because they come together, it irrevocably changes their lives. I'm not going to tell you any more because you can find that out when you eventually see it.

Now let's think about the motion picture *Titanic (1997)*. The character that was written as Rose (also played by Kate Winslet), within the reality of the film – was part of an arranged marriage and her life was like that of a bird in a cage. Then she has that short relationship the Jack the artist (played by Leonardo DiCaprio). I'm saying short because it's really only a day and a half and then – the ship—you know – (points down.)

(Audience laughter)

Right? I mean it wasn't like they were hanging out together for a long time. That's why I picked it. Rose has an affair with an artist, a love affair and he paints her picture in the nude – but it's not about that. What it **is about... because they (Rose and Jack) were together, Rose's life changed.** And the very last scene of the movie – you see it. I remember reading the screenplay at the end of the movie shows Rose (as the older woman) first throwing the precious stone back into the ocean. I don't know if I would have done that...

(Audience laughter)

So she throws the diamond back into the ocean? What's that about? She could have sold it and got a nice oceanfront condo in Boca... or someplace?

(Audience laughter)

Anyway, she throws the diamond back into the sea. The next time we see her in the present frame, she is lying still in her cabin. And I thought (when I saw the film) is she dead? Did she die after living a full life and is now finally back together with everyone who perished on the Titanic? Or... is she sleeping... in peace? James Cameron, wrote this in his screenplay:

> A graceful pan across Rose's shelf of carefully arranged pictures.
>
> Rose as a young actress in California, radiant... a theatrically lit studio publicity shot... Rose and her husband, with their two children... Rose with her son at his college graduation... Rose with her children and grandchildren at her 70th birthday. A collage of images of a life lived well.
>
> THE PAN STOPS on an image filling frame. Rose, circa 1920. She is at the beach, sitting on

a horse at the surf line. The Santa Monica pier, with its rollercoaster is behind her. She is grinning, full of life.

We PAN OFF the last picture to Rose herself, warm in her bunk. A profile shot. She is very still. She could be sleeping, or maybe something else.

And so Cameron is saying, Rose had a full wonderful life because of that almost momentary relationship with Jack the artist. And whether she is dead or sleeping is really up to you… and that's where he leaves it. And I thought, two characters come together for a very short period of time (and they do get a lot done).

(Audience laughter)

And because these two characters come together in the way they do changes Rose's entire life. Instead of being forced into an arranged marriage (like a caged bird) she lives a full and wonderful life. In that sense, the last shot of the film visually gave us the entire story in one pan of the camera.

So, here are the modes of expression of character or character frames that can originate from your novel or short story

The Pitch
The Script

Now, one other thing, when you're developing a character. Let's go with the first ten pages. What if you are writing for television? Trying to develop your novel into a television series or mini series? It's different. You don't have to do the whole job in the first ten pages because most characters in television are a slow roll. You will have the opportunity to flesh out characters in smaller parts. But with that said, you still have to create the most important character elements in the pilot. That's the initial episode of a series where the audience is introduced to the main characters and the major framework for the show that is to follow.

Since this lecture was given in 2009, many producers and television outlets have decided to do away with pilots all together and produce a limited version of the series from the start. A production such as *House of Cards (2013)* initially had a limited number of episodes made available to the Netflix subscribers all at one time. They abandoned the idea of a pilot or serial broadcast.

Network television still uses the serial format, but now in television shows such as *The Black List (2013) The Knick (2014) and Chicago PD (2014)* major characters or what the audience perceives as major/regular characters in the show are killed of routinely. The writers develop these characters in the traditional manner and just when the audience thinks they know them, they are eliminated. So, your development of character within this medium again must be front-loaded. Get the most interesting/compelling aspects of your character out there early because you may not have twenty episodes or several seasons to flush them out on the fly. You might think, why spend a lot of time developing a character that you will eliminate? My answer, would you do it any differently in a book? I don't think so. And I think anytime you can engage "pull in" your audience with interesting characters, you should do it. Think of William Shakespeare and characters like the Nurse or the Apothecary in Romeo and Juliet. Think about how Shakespeare presented them within the story. He made them interesting and vital to what was going on. You should do the same.

What if you write for the Internet? You adapt your novel as a serial episodic to be shown in smaller segments on the Internet. In this case, you may be developing this on your own and not writing a script for anyone other than yourself. Does this actually work? I mean in the big picture? Does anyone take anything shot for the Internet seriously? The answer is "yes" and "no" depending upon your production values. If your work looks like it's been shot in your backyard with louse light and sound. No one is going to take it seriously. However, if you spend a little time in creating acceptable production values, you can get a following for your work. As far as character development, that all depends how you present it. If it is serial, then you can do a slow roll a little bit at a time, if it were feature format I would front load the first ten minutes and grab your audience. You can produce your story as a mini series, which is a combination of the two formats. But… what can you really do with it?

Here's what I think. If you get enough traction with it and get lots of visits to your site, that can translate into something tangible that you can cite in a fuller pitch meeting. If your project has a lot of heat, people will take an interest. You could also, produce a nice expanded trailer for your book. This really is a marketing tool, very much like they would do in a movie theatre. Show them "how" the film could be if it were made. Get it off the page and visualize your idea. That's a great topic for another seminar!

(Audience laughter)

So depending upon where or how you present your book and characters you will have to be connected the method in which you present it. This means, that not every presentation of one idea will be the same. You have to connect to and reach your reader or viewer by connecting them to your character. You want them to care what happens next. If you produce it yourself, let's say for the Internet, the outcome will be smaller, but you will have more control. The hardest part, I think in this transition from fiction to film… we have to talk about this.

Fiction… you are the only person writing and when you publish you will work with one person – your editor. And when you get to the television or film medium it becomes truly a collaborative effort – and that could become an issue that can affect the final outcome of the way your project looks. It could actually be better than you ever believed or… it could be worse than your worst nightmare.

Let's say that you are fortunate enough to get your novel into the hands of Anthony Hopkins and he or his designee reads it... then you get it back with notes for certain changes or additions that would have to occur if he were to attach himself to the project. In this case, your writing becomes part of a collaborative effort and you have to be open to that. Also, by the time your novel is transformed into a screenplay and then shooting script (after the input of designers, stars, producers and others) it's going to change and like any relationship – you have to give and take a little bit. But you have to make sure that you don't lose your way and your final script doesn't become something else. You'll say that's not what I wrote. But by that time, it will be too late.

One of my plays was produced in (I'm not going to say the name to protect the guilty). It was a fully professional production that's all I will say. When I read the reviews – it got great reviews. It is a tale of father and daughter jealousy and cruelty. The father becomes so jealous of his daughter (both are painters) that he breaks her hands in a paint box so she cannot paint anymore. Despite this, she goes on and become s a world famous artist. The play takes place at her mother's funeral when she (now a famous painter who has gone dry) comes home (from Paris) and sees her father (now an old man) for the first time. Without telling you the whole story, the old man wants her to forgive him for what he has done to her. At the end of the play, she cannot but does understand why he did what he did. She goes back to Paris understanding why he did what he did and is able to paint again. I didn't write it this way... it's better than that.

(Audience laughter)

The producer of the play thinks "We can't have that at the end of the production. She has to forgive him and send the audience out the door feeling good about what they saw." So in that production which I will not name, the ending was changed and she forgives her father and takes him back to Paris with her! So now I'm reading the reviews, which said something, like "The play *Autumn Sweet* is a poignant drama but chokes at the conclusion with a "Hollywood" ending." I said to myself "I didn't write that!"

(Audience laughter)

The producer changed the ending of my play and I got nailed for it. Why? Because I was on a ski trip in Tahoe instead of being where I should have been. At the opening of my play. I was invited but did not go.

(Audience laughter)

The point of this story is that you need to go with the flow – collaborate – but stay true to your core idea, your characters, and your story. Yes, give and take but not to the extent that you lose your original idea or in my case the ending.

6

Adaptation – Your First Ten Script Pages

Description, Action and Dialogue
Writing Great Characters in the First Ten Pages

You may be writing for a reader, a producer or an audience and you have got to give. And I've we stated before, that's where the ten pages come in. you have to create a hook in the beginning and once they are on board, they you can roll out any way you need to roll out. How do you get to this with character? Three ways. **Description, Action and Dialogue.** Essentially on the screen that boils down to what they do what they say, how they look, and what other characters say about them and the physical world they exist within. Your main character may say wonderful things about themselves, but they could be telling a lie. You have to show the truth. Let's talk about **DESCRIPTION.**

So, how is the best way to describe your characters in those first ten pages where your character has their initial introduction to the story? Right? So, you have to introduce them in a compelling way. In your novel you could and can take all the time you need. Went to boarding school in France, studied law – add little anecdotes. You don't have that much time and space in a screenplay. You have to cut to the chase.

INTERIOR – LIBRARY – DAY

Professor Muldoon, a crusty but benign college professor, dressed in tweed and loafers, holds an old book tightly as he hobbles down a long oak stairway into the the living room of the old English manor.

You do it all in one to three lines not a page and a half. That's it, you have to create the same impact that you would generate in a page and half description you might have in your novel. And Anthony Hopkins acts it out.

(Audience laughter)

Let's talk about that. Shall we? In your novel you have every detail covered so that you know who the characters are in every detail. Now you've got a screenplay and its all got to be in there but at around 120 pages. So you cut, but you don't want to strip everything out of it. You must capture the essence of your full character description that's in your book. What I'm saying is that you must keep the soul of your book alive and you get that 50 or 100 word description and you boil it down to five or ten words and that's the challenge. But, don't be a good soldier that writes their screenplay in 100 pages but in doing so; the end product has no life in it. You must keep the soul of your book alive and so you struggle to make sure you get in those five or ten lines of description that you don't lose any calories. It has to have the same fullness. The next element is ACTION.

Action is how your character moves in the space – the universe you have created for them. You don't have to write "He walked slowly put one foot after another." You don't have to do that. Instead focus on something interesting about how your character does something. Some sort of interesting action that they do like the way they tie their tie (James Bond) pet a cat (The Godfather) or walk on a sidewalk (Jack Nicholson in (AS GOOD AS IT GETS). But you can create action as it happens "on the fly" as your character does it. Do you remember the old television series *Columbo (1968)*?

(Audience laughter)

I can't believe you guys remember that? Okay, well you would want to put a little bit about that character's actions in your set up. And Detective Columbo was interesting to us because we always enjoyed the way he seemed to physically fumble through each situation he was in. There was a "fumbling" almost inept quality about the character that made his adversaries not take him very seriously. They though "this guy is a total

dork." But we loved to see Columbo fumble through and solve every crime despite how carefully it was planned. Sherlock Holmes is the flip side, the Victorian side. Holmes is very formal, scientific and he observes using his five senses everything intently. All his fastidious actions come into play, So action is important because it shows something about your character's way of existing physically in their universe that makes them interesting and worthy of our time. And we can go through all sorts of things to achieve that.

(Off stage Voice)

Ten minutes? Are you sure?

(Audience laughter)

In the writing class we did yesterday, we were improvising about the "space between people." Just the space can change the way your characters react to things within their universe. You know those people in New York City on the subway? The subway car is packed – standing room only – and they are this far away from one another.)

(Catalano moves very close to a male audience member – almost touches)

(Audience laughter)

Don't worry, I won't touch you...

(Audience laughter)

Unless you want me to?

(Audience laughter.)

They are this far away and it's not a problem. Try that in Los Angeles. Try to move that close to someone and see what happens. I was on line the other day at a store (waiting to check out) and some guy (who was in a hurry) came up right behind me. He very close, I could feel him breathing on me and pressing up against my butt.

(Audience laughter)

No nothing like that... he was (I assume) trying to get the line to move faster. I turned to him and said pressing up against me is not going to make the checkout person or the line any faster. He just moved back... no comment. Now the definition of personal space in Los Angeles and now is different let's say than riding the subway in New York City during the rush hour. This guy pressing up against me in line was a violation of my personal space while it might not have even been noticeable in another situation. Definition of space in Ohio, Los Angeles is different than in New York City, Tokyo or Paris. You can create visual element for your character before they even say one word. This really goes to my example of Meryl Streep in DOUBT. That kind of visual introduction says something about your character and how they move – that might take you several pages to achieve in a novel.

I recently attended a screening of the film *Chef (2014)* that (without giving anything away here) is about a chef. The opening sequence of the film (as music plays) is a series of visual shots our main character preparing food – doing the slicing, dicing – all the things a chef would do. But this action was not casual, he was preparing with a sense of purpose – so you knew right away, even before the first word of dialogue was spoken that the meal he was preparing was an important one. He wasn't just cooking breakfast for himself... it was more than that – much more. You'll have to see the film, because you're not getting anything else out of me on CHEF. Have any of you seen it?

(Audience laughter)

Really, we should stop right now and all go to the movies!

(Audience laughter)

But we can't can we? Can we? So you want to open with your characters up front and make them interesting and compelling within that first ten pages or ten minutes of screening. You want the reader/audience to want to know more about them and why they are doing what they are doing. So ACTION is very important tool for you to use to connect your characters to your audience. The other element that is important is of course DIALOGUE.

DIALOGUE is important because it is one the ways (probably one of the most important) a character communicates with an audience and other characters in your story. Dialogue is one of the primary ways your audience gets to know all the things they need to know to be connected to the story. Also, dialogue can reveal things about the character themselves; do they have a dialect, what do they say about themselves, what do they say about others, are they always telling the truth or do they lie? How do they speak? Do they speak in shortened phrases like?

(Catalano does Joe Pesci imitation from the film *Good Fellas – 1990*)

"You said I was funny? Funny like I'm a clown, I amuse you? I make you laugh? I'm here to amuse you? What do you mean funny, funny how? How am I funny?"

(Audience laughter)

That's one way of doing it. Or does your character speak in long-winded speeches like let's say Sherlock Holmes. Figure out how what they say and how they say it fits in to what you are trying to accomplish.

You can ask my brother just one simple question and he will go off for an hour or more on it. So, really, I don't like asking him anything… you know.

(Audience laughter)

"Hey, Bro… "I call him "Bro" which is term of endearment. "How was your day?" Then he looks at me and smiles as if to say I so glad you asked. "Well, I got up this morning, brushed my teeth and then after that…" I think to myself… please just the highlights – do you have to tell me everything?

Is this your character? So, how they speak dialogue is just as important as exposition and content. When you finally finish the introduction of your main character, I am assuming that your main character is going to be there. Right? So your character walks in and I don't know we were doing *The Sopranos* yesterday. I kind of dressed for it today. Your character walks in on page two and speaks for the first time with a Jersey dialect: "How ya'doin?"

(Catalano moves)

And he moves within the space leading with chin and is hunched over a bit (like he's going to whisper something important in your ear) or your main character could be an attorney with a physically that is more upright (morally driven)

(Catalano moves again this time more upright and driven.)

"How are you today?"

No chest, no chin. Little details like play strongly or should I say visually. You bring over the characteristics of your novel but with less stated. You keep your character's quality; you don't lose it with abbreviation. It's just as detailed but the detail has been compressed into Description, Action and Dialogue. Guess what? All of these elements are visual and auditory. You have moved from an intellectual medium (your novel) where everything is happens and is created in your head (your imagination) to a primarily visual medium based in external stimuli.

So, you wouldn't say your character enters leading with his chin and right foot. This type of physicality is too clinical. You might instead describe it using visual metaphors. Something like "Joey G walks in the room like a predator ready to strike with his eyes focused on the prize." The metaphor compresses it all into one short section and you can come up with a much better metaphor than I just made up on the spot.

(Audience laughter)

Then, the cinematographer, actors and directors can see it as you see it (from your words) and use their own creative input to interpret it. You might be thinking, what if they interpret my writing in a way that is different than my interpretation? Interpretation is never going to be exact. You aren't going to like this, but often the different interpretations make the impact of the work better. As we have said before, as long as the spirit of your original work is intact, you're okay. And that's what you want to set up in the first ten pages.

7

Wrapping It Up

Writing Great Characters in the First Ten Pages

ULTIMATELY, YOU WANT to introduce your characters in an interesting way and as soon as possible (that is a plot device) put them in some sort of peril or heighten the stakes.

This is what I liked so much about the film I won't tell you about – you know *The Chef (2014)*. The stakes are heightened right from the first minutes of the film. I was pulled into the main characters almost immediately. Also think about the other examples we've mentioned like JURASIC PARK – you know within the first three or four minutes of the film that this is going to be one rocket ride of a story and character. Make the reader
fall in love with your characters and then put them in peril. Threaten to take them away and then you have the whole script to get them out of it.

Never forget your audience. Pull them in as soon as possible and take them on a journey. Whatever you do, don't save the best for last. Not going to work here. Don't roll out the most compelling elements of your characters in the intermission or act break – do it up front.

Remember, we live in a society where everyone wants it right away. Some writers even do it in the first page! Novelists do it as well. They create very compelling characters on the first page – so someone picking up the book for the first time will hesitate to put it down. Also, remember film and television are visual mediums – a director will want to show your story more than they will want to tell it. Your screenplay will be blocked into a series of visual setups – focused for a visual telling of the story on a screen.

In your first ten pages that, hook the reader right up front with a heightened reality. If you don't get them up front – you may not be able to get them later.

Thank you very much.

(Audience applause)

WRITING ON YOUR FEET

Improvisational Techniques for Writers
Part 1

SAN DIEGO STATE UNIVERSITY
25th Annual Writers Conference

WORKSHOP TRANSCRIPT
HOW TO ADAPT YOUR NOVEL INTO A SCREENPLAY

BOOK 2

Frank Catalano

8

Writing on Your Feet

Writing on Your Feet

TODAY'S SEMINAR IS called WRITING ON YOUR FEET and it's just a quick (you know) catchy title for utilizing improvisational techniques for writing or adaptation of your literary work (novel) into a screenplay. Many actors use improvisation to help them create characters and dialogue. However, many writers are reticent to get up out of their chairs and put their work "on its feet" because they are trained to do all of their creating mentally. This is fine. But as a writer I wanted to say that using the improvisational approach—I mean actually getting up and "doing" instead of "sitting" engages all of your senses. Why? To give you a better understanding of your story and the characters that live in the universe you have created.

Yesterday, we were having a discussion about a play that I had written. I had an offer to publish it but I hadn't read it in a very long while and wanted to look at it one more time before I was going to put it in print. Why? Because time had passed, I wanted to see if the work still did what I thought it did for an audience when I first created it. So, my way of accomplishing this was to put it up on its feet. Of course, I could have sit down in my living room and read it again – but I want to engage all of my senses. This was my answer. It worked for me.

And it can work for you as well. This putting on its feet and read aloud can assist all of us whether you are a fiction writer or a screenwriter – it serves you to experience your work on multiple levels – and be on its feet, read aloud by actors And, we're in Los Angeles (San Diego) there with so many actors available that would be glad to help you do just that.

So, I decided to have a staged reading and put my play up on its feet and watch and listen to it (instead of read it.) That's what I did. And it was very helpful for me. I listened, watched, made notes and some revisions. I found it to be a short cut way of getting to the core of what the play was about and what I was trying to say to my audience. And so when we write, we engage our senses.

When you are sitting and you are writing on your laptop or perhaps a legal pad (everyone has their own method), you visualize your characters and hear their voices in your mind. Isn't that true? Have you ever heard of the Italian playwright Luigi Pirandello? One of his most famous plays is *Six Characters in Search of an Author…* a very good play. Pirandello had the hardest time writing because of his jealous wife. When he wrote, he would like himself in his studio to write so his wife couldn't disturb him. His way of writing was to speak his character's voices out loud and when he did, his wife (hearing voices through the locked door) was convinced that he had a woman in the studio with him. She would often pound on the door while he was trying to write. Not an easy way to write, but Pirandello believed, as a writer, that this method was an effective way of creating characters and story for his plays. What about putting your characters on their feet?

What about putting your characters on their feet with little or no written material? Some of you are thinking, "I just have an idea, nothing else but an idea. How can my characters get up and talk? They are not fully developed. How can they or I say anything? I can't do it." I say, "yes you can" and that's exactly what you are going to do today. I want to explore putting your characters on their feet and letting them talk (they could actually be sitting too – it doesn't matter). I want you to be able to listen to them, watch them move and learning. No takers? So, even if I got two of you today and I place you within an improvisational scene within your idea – you provide the idea, the characters and we will let the characters play it out? What do you think? Remember, the writer doesn't have to write down every single word his/her characters say – they may not all work. But what you can get is an understanding of your characters, how they might relate and how they move within their universe. Also, it is really helpful to improvise the same scenario (idea) several times? What happens then?

What happens is a magical little thing… truth. I don't know if you can put your finger on it but the truth (of your idea) kind of floats to the top… and what I mean by that is that the underlying meaning starts to reveal itself as it is experienced by a larger number of people. We could have fifty or sixty people in this room form groups and send them to several corners of this hotel (so they can see or hear what is happening in here). Then bring them in one group at a time and have them improvise the same exact scenario (idea). The result? There will be repetition and there will be differences in each group's improvisation. However, there will be certain qualities, themes, characteristics that will be evident in most or all. What comes out of the experiment is that the idea has a universal through line or truth that can be see in whole or part in all of the improvisations. If there is conflict within it with a certain kind of resolution and you say, "Okay, then, that's the way it will be. I'm going to incorporate that element into my idea or maybe I'm not going in the right direction. None of the improvisations reflect my idea at all."

Improvisation can be a tool that you can use to work within a framed scenario…

(Catalano hand an email list by audience member)

Thank you. … or idea to take it to the next level. When you are under a lot of pressure to write, you know you have to have the project in by a certain deadline.

9

Writing Using Moving Pictures

Writing on your Feet

DURING THE *ROBOTECH* series, the writing and production (all of it) happened all at once. There was always a looming deadline hanging over our heads. To make matters worse, the writers and the actors for that matter during the making of the show were never really totally sure of what it was about. Like the CIA, we were just given small parts to work on and never really got a sense of the whole. This was not in anyway a nefarious plot to hide some dark secret from all of us. It was just the crazy nature of how that show came together. The big picture was really only known by one person, the shows producer the late Carl Macek (1951 – 2010). Carl had a creative vision for the show as a whole and had a sense of how the story was going to play out and would summarize each episode's footage. Remember, the show was being written to already existing animated footage. What the writers wrote had to fit that footage; they couldn't just write whatever they wanted. But the challenge was, what to write within that footage and to make sure it all fit as a whole. We used to call Carl Macek "the chees master" because he could look at a small clip or a whole episode in Japanese and then spin off (with extreme detail) what was going on in that particular episode and how it all fit in to the larger mosaic. For the rest of us... not Carl people... it was Japanese anime and we had very little to go on except the visual components of what we were looking at.

To write a *Robotech* episode, you would start with a plot summary (there was also a show Bible) and a twenty-two minute episode that had been time coded so that you can write the dialogue and effects in sync. One way to do it was to read the summary, and then try to figure out how to get that done ahead of time as if you were writing a script for a movie. But that really (in my opinion) doesn't work because you have got to consider the footage. Remember, you are only writing the dialogue and reactions. Pretty easy... right?

Let me say, writing for anime is not for the faint hearted. You have got to be true to the characters (or the fans will fry you) and you have got to put words in the character's mouths that fit. The real challenge is to try to find words that makes sense and at the same time fit into the characters moving mouths. If it were not written "in sync" then it would have to be written correctly in the studio by the director... trust me you don't want that to happen.

A second method is to understand the framework of the story as stated in the summary. Know where you are going and where you have to end up and then let the characters tell you what they are saying. What I mean by this is essentially writing on your feet. Let the physicality of the characters determine what they say. It's a lot easier, because you are not burdened by the structure of a preexisting script. Sometimes having a script is harder than "not" having a script. Once in a while, on some shows, we would get scripts written in English directly from Tokyo and they would be literal translations like "Hey watch it man or I will beat you into many pulps!"

(Audience laughter)

Even with their script, you have no story. Well you actually have less than a story so you are better off throwing the literal translation out and let the characters do the talking. Just play the footage and start talking for the characters as they move through the frames. What happens then? At some point the story and the characters start to emerge clearly and a framework is established. The same process happens with you view a movie with subtitles. In the beginning you read every word and then after a while you begin to understand character and situation over and above what is being written in the subtitle. Now, my experience with letting my characters talk has only one problem, sometimes they sound like me and say things that maybe I would say. This happens a lot in the dubbing studio when you are working very late at night... you are tired and suddenly your not voicing what is written but instead putting in your own "very in sync" lines. During the *Robotech* series, my character Rand is in the middle of an Invid invasion when he rides his version of a motorcycle up to another character's mother and says something (I don't remember what was actually written) but I said, and it fit perfectly "GET A JOB." We recorded the correct line as well but somehow GET A JOB made it to the final cut and was aired as part of the show when it played on television. Of course, the *Robotech* fans, were not fooled for a minute and knew it was a mistake... but the fact is, the line still remains today and when I see *Robotech* fans, they ask me to autograph their pictures with "Get a job..."

So the immense power of writing on your feet is evident. But I will give you another example that is even sillier than GET A JOB. I was writing and co producing a series called *The Adventures of Dynamo Duck* for **FOX KID'S NETWORK**. I was part of a writing team that had to convert over three hundred hours of raw animal footage based upon the French film maker Jean Tourane's idea for a children's television series *Saturnin le canard* about the duckling Saturnin who had all kinds of adventures. The series was produced using real animals, dressed up with sunglasses, hats and other props that lived inside a miniature world. A small duck was the main character, fighting crimes of the evil Dr. Mortek (a monkey) and other assorted villains. The animals wander around on miniature sets with scale models of trucks and other vehicles. The duck's name was changed to "Dynamo Duck."

(Audience laughter)

Remember, this was not "wild life" footage – this was a duck wearing a bow tie driving a little car and or flying a biplane. None of the animals were hurt – nothing like that. But this series was totally written on its feet!

(Audience laughter)

Basically, our first step was take all the raw animal footage and cut into smaller workable sections. We did this in a studio at my home doing what they called back then "paper cuts" and then would assemble the raw material into actual episodes. I think we did about two hundred of them. Each episode had the same reoccurring characters (ducks, gerbils, frogs, goldfishes, weasels) but each had a different stand-alone storyline. Almost all of the writing was done "on its feet" working off the visual images that were contained in the footage that was cut for each episode. There was no way we could, apart from the footage, come up with "gags" or setups with payoffs at the end as you would in a traditional script. Also, remember, we had to tell a story. There had to be a narrative structure with a beginning middle and end. My writing partner for this project, Gregory Snegoff worked for hours creating what finally became the basis for all cut footage and dialogue spoken for each episode. After we created the framework, we gave some of the episodes to other writers to complete specific "in sync" sections of dialogue. You may be wondering "How do you write "in sync" dialogue to a duck or a gerbil?" That is a seminar all into itself and Greg Snegoff is the master at putting words or sounds in the mouths of just about anything you could imagine. An example for the Dynamo Duck character, the actual duck used in the filming (there were probably several) would from time to time shake his head. We wrote actual lines every time the duck would move his mouth (no computers here) and then (no matter when) if the duck shook his head, we would insert a "sheesh" to the line. Here we are working directly off of the visual image. So the visual image is the key.

There was one episode that featured a whole group of little yellow ducklings waddling about, dressed in little pirate hats. So, we decided to use the footage we had and do a pirate story. We cut the footage and wrote a short summary of the storyline that should go with it. All a scriptwriter had to do was write dialogue. The writer who was assigned came back a few days later and said, "I can't do this anymore!"

(Audience laughter)

"I don't know what to write? I've used my three pirate jokes and now I don't know what else I could write for them to say?" My reply? Stop thinking in terms of literal narrative (duck jokes or pirate jokes) (he was in fact an excellent writer) with a setup and pay off. Just watch the footage and let it lead you to a situation and the rest will take care of itself. Writing on your feet is a moment-to-moment kind of a thing. That's the best approach to this sort of writing. Because he had written the same way all his life, he just couldn't grasp it and many writers approach their work in the same manner.

And so my point is, sometimes we have this overall concept of something we want to tell and we can't do it because we are locked into the idea itself and don't know where to start. How many times have we had the blank page and no matter what we right we say to ourselves over and over again…"no that's no good" "no that's not right…" Instead, think about just taking it moment to moment. It could be a simple little thing we you start with a situation where two characters come into a space. And that's all you've got to start with. The say, "Hi how are you?" Your two characters are on a bus stop and one of them is a CIA agent. Then, Go! And all of a sudden the two begin to connect and react to one another in that simple space. One speaks, then the other back and forth back and forth. Now, out of that exchange a couple of things can happen.

One, it totally dissolves into "nothing." That's part of being an artist. Two, it can begin to formalize and become something else. It flowers. But it becomes something totally different. Your CIA agent and the person they meet by chance at a bus stop fall in love. And now all of a sudden, it's a love story. And you go, "Whoa, okay? I'll take that." Then you start building it from there.

10

WRITING USING YOUR FIVE SENSES

Writing on your Feet

So, WHEN WE get up and start moving our characters, it gives us some opportunities. Number one, we can listen to them engaging our sense of hearing. Now, every one of us has a different sensory order. We all have five senses, but some of our senses are stronger for us, than others. How many of you think that? How many of you think that your senses are not equal?

(Audience reacts.)

So I would personally say that I am more of a "visual" person than a listener. So, I might remember what you look like but I may not remember your name. I can say that I am visually oriented. Second place for me would be "touch." So I like to touch things a lot when I shop… and after that maybe "smell." Listening for me is probably on the bottom of the list. My wife often says to me, "You know you never listen to a word I say!" and I respond, "What?"

(Audience laughter)

Now I know you are going to say that's a guy thing. Maybe and maybe not and sometimes you can create characters that are of different sensory centers. For example, a female character tells her male lover, "You never tell me you love me." And the guy responds, "What are you talking about? I washed your car yesterday!" So she's saying I want to "hear" you "I'm auditory" while he's thinking, "I'm visual baby; here's your car, I cleaned it. I could have been watching TV."

How many have heard this? The male character says to his female lover, "I love you so much!" and she snaps back at him "Don't tell me you love me... show me... stop drinking with your buds every night."

It can work both ways. When we put our characters on their feet, we are engaging all of our senses instead of just doing it all in our head. We are engaging auditory, touch, maybe smell... let me ask you this... in your own universe, and do certain places have specific smells attached to them? And don't those individual smell sometimes evoke certain emotions or memories for you?

(Audience member, "Oh, yeah... yeah.")

I used to live in Hawaii (there's a certain floral smell about that place) and I'm not talking about people working at the lei stands waiting for you when you get off the plane. No not that... Hawaii has a certain smell to it (like gardenias) that is unique and I could be walking at the mall in Los Angeles – somebody will walk by and they are wearing a gardenia type of perfume and it takes me right back to Hawaii. New York has a smell too... actually more than a couple of smells.

(Audience laughter)

and some of them...

(Audience laughter – audience member comment)

There is a smell in New York which I will never forget smelling as a child when my father drove over the Kosciuszko Bridge which was a truss bridge connecting New York City's boroughs of Brooklyn and Queens. When we drove over it the smell was something like rotten eggs mixed with a dead animal. It was horrible. My dad told me that we were driving by a meat processing plant and that's why it smelled so bad. And now as an adult, when I smell something even remotely like that I am right back there, a child again in the back of my dad's car, going over the Kosciuszko Bridge!

(Audience laughter)

So, smell does have a way... not that I'm saying we should spray ourselves.

(Catalano acknowledges audience member)

Yes? You were going to say something... I thought you were waving at me?

(Audience laughter)

What about auditory? We hear our characters... and what about touch? We watch how our characters respond physically to one another... we watch how they touch one another. We can also experience a visual picture as two characters relate physically that tells us the story. If two characters enter a space and you are writing them, let's use our example of the CIA agent and at the bus stop.

(Catalano approaches an audience member to illustrate)

(Audience laughter)

Don't worry... I won't actually touch you.

(Audience member laughs)

I am playing your role and I sit down and I do this...

(Catalano assumes a specific physicality – sits very close but doesn't touch.)

And you go, "Wait I've never thought of this. The CIA agent, ever so slightly, touches her. What does this mean? That's for you to fill in with dialogue and narrative.
Forget about writing it… all you have to do is observe what is around you… that's what actors do. Why was I sitting so close? Maybe, I was passing a small data chip to her… or maybe, I am trying to assassinate her. Let the characters on their feet create the visual picture and physicality while you fill in the rest with dialogue. And by the way, this is not fiction… this is real.

I sat on a crowded train once in New York and there was a guy reading a newspaper standing very close to me as the train moved.

(Catalano stands close to an audience member but doesn't touch them.)

He was like this.

(Catalano moves closer to the audience member but doesn't touch him)

While he never actually touched me, which was pretty hard to do since the moving train was tossing us back and forth, he was able to get close enough to smell me. I thought I smelled okay for that time of day.

(Audience laughter)

But this guy reeked to stale cigarettes smoke and mothballs. Not a very fragrant combination. We were so close to each other that you could barely put a sheet of paper between us. And yet, we did not speak or acknowledge on another. One could argue that the universe that they move within governs the distance between two people on a crowded train. That is… the train is crowded and so complete strangers exist, not acknowledging one another at all even though they are less than one inch apart. Maybe because they are so close, they can smell one another. One reeks of stale cigarettes and beer; the other of cheap cologne. What does that say about each character and how can you explain this? It can only be explained by the nature of the physical universe they live in. Now take this same scenario and move it to a place like Los Angeles. I was on line and a supermarket and I'm waiting on line and some guy is behind me… the check out person was moving **very slowly.**

(Catalano motions the check out person – audience laughter)

You know, one of those things. And the guy standing behind me has moved right up against me trying to make the line go faster. And the way he decided he was going to do that was to move up real close breathe down my neck and brush up against my butt. He did it once, then again and then a third time when I finally turned around and looked at him: "Don't touch my butt! It's not going to make the check out person move any faster." I felt that he was invading my space because in Los Angeles, where we are in our cars all the time and not closely packed together in trains – the amount of personal space we assume is much larger. If this same person were that close to me on a crowded train, maybe it would have been appropriate. So this is all part of writing on your feet.

All of this comes into play when you write this way. This heightened feedback and not all of it is going to be useable. Some of it is not going to work for your story. So, this method is going to tell you what to leave out as well. It is merely an experimental exploration that will provide to you a multitude of choices. You may say to yourself, "I like this, let's see where it takes me." Or "I don't like this so I will not go in that direction." It's a wonderful way to start your adaptation to a screenplay or your book. Take two characters or even one character and place them in a situation (the who, what, when and where) and then see what they do. Let the characters and the universe you have created for them take you on a journey. In a moment, we are going to try a few of these.

11

Manipulation versus Selection

Writing on your Feet

You can, as a writer, participate within an improvisation. But many of you sitting here today probably don't want to do that. You say to yourself, "I don't want to get up, I am not an actor." Or "I don't want to improvise my idea to a room full of writers." This is not a problem. If you are shy and you don't like getting on your feet, get actors to do it for you. If you don't want to share your idea, you can start your story from scratch or you can define a specific who, what, where or when. So if I said to you I have absolutely no idea about what I want to write about. I have no story. I have no characters... in short, I have nothing. But, I'm going to get two people and put them somewhere and create their physicality and maybe the universe they inhabit and start them off with just a word. Not even an important word... just a word... maybe something like "rosebud." That's it. I start the improvisation with that and from that starting point you go. You might have on your first page "CIA agent walks up to a bus stop and sits down next to a woman carrying a small leather bag close to her, like a rare book. He sits down very close to her (just like we have done today) and just says one word, "rosebud." You may wonder what does that mean? You don't have to know. Once the characters begin reacting to one another the meaning of "rosebud" begins to emerge. Then, you try the same setup with two different people and experience that situation as it evolves. There may be similar qualities or the situation may go in an entirely different direction. As the writer or creator, you use a process of selection rather than mental manipulation. What am I saying here? What is manipulation?

In writing, the process of manipulation is when the writer creates all of the details of any given situation. Every detail of what happens is written in and every outcome is carefully controlled. Then what of selection?

The writer creates a framework to develop the idea and through experimentation "selects" from what what organically evolves what will become the permanent story.

This method has its pitfalls. A lot of your experimentation may result in failure. It may also take your story and characters in a direction that was not intended. But it will also take you on a journey where you can discover elements of story and character that (although inside of you) that you would have utilized. The skill of selection is to take what you can from your experimentation that works and discard those elements that don't. But it is not wasted – you also learn from what does not work. This is writing on your feet.

12

Writing Using Improvisation

Writing on your Feet

I WAS GOING TO do what I call "TAG SCENES" Let me tell you what a "TAG SCENE" is so that you can use this technique on your own. A "TAG SCENE" is this… okay lets' try one so you can see what I'm talking about. Okay, everybody, let's get up… you need a group maybe five or ten people, put them in a circle. Let's make the circle a bit larger so we have lots of space to move. We start with just a circle.

> (Catalano selects an audience member as a volunteer and both move to the center of the circle.)

Let's start with you and I. I will start the improvisation and you will respond. I speak and then you speak… and we move and as the scenario develops at some point one of you (indicating audience members) will say, "FREEZE." The two people in the middle of the circle literally freeze what ever they are doing. Their physicality and speech becomes literally frozen as if they were mannequins in a store window. Then the person who stated "freeze" will come into the center of the circle and "tag" on of the two people out – then assume the exact physical stance and gesture they were in. The person tagged returns to the outer circle and can come back in again at any time What happens then, is that person, who comes in, assuming the physical gesture, breaks it and begins a whole new improvisation with a whole new who, what when and where. A totally new situation is created with a different physicality and characters until they are "frozen" by one of you. Then the improvisation ends and a new one is created by the person coming in. The entire process continues over and over again. New characters, new situations created in an endless loop. Pretty crazy eh? A couple of things to remember:

The two people in the center of the circle must be able to create a specific who, what, when and where before they are tagged out. This means, that one person can come in and say one line then gets tagged out. We have to allow them to create the basics.

When the incoming person creates a certain reality, the person already in the circle must accept it. This means if one person comes in and tags someone out, then says (as part of the new scene) "Can you press the thirteen floor for me please." And the person that already in the circles responds with "What do you mean, thirteenth floor? We are at the beach!" This would create a disconnect and the scene would be hard to create because the participants were not listening to on another.

A word about "physicality." When the person comes in and tags someone out, they must create their situation out of the physical gesture (from the person they tagged out) they have assumed. They should not, assume it then drop it and say their first line. The first line has to evolve out of the physical gesture.

Okay? Should we try a few of these?

(Nervous Audience laughter.)

I'll start. Let me say one more thing to you.

(Catalano directs his comments to the audience member with him in the middle of the circle.)

It's important that you and I are a bit "over physical." Meaning we should use larger gestures to provide specific gestures to assume for the people tagging us out and starting a new improvisation. Okay, should we try it?

> (Audience member Yes!)

Okay, don't leave me up here... one of you guys has to tag me out. Okay?

> (Audience member "We will tag you out after like twenty five minutes" More audience laughter.)

You can tag me out or anyone else. It doesn't matter. All of that... okay, here we go.
Oh wait a minute.

> (A new person (female), not in the seminar, enters the room.)

Hi.

> (Person "I feel like I'm literally walking in on writing on your feet. Did I just hear you say that I can come in?"

I did. Why don't you watch this for a second and then join us?

> (Person responds, "Okay...")

Have you ever done improvisation?

> (Person responds: "Oh... I hate it... but I'll watch.)

Improvisation for writers... it just clears the house out.

> (Audience laughter.)

Okay, here we go – one, two, three...

(Improvisation begins Audience #1 is female)

Catalano: "I'm really sorry I'm late honey…"

Audience #1: "I fixed your favorite meal… you always have an excuse."

Catalano: "I had to work at the office… look I mean I've got a microphone."

Audience #1: "You always have to work…"

Catalano: "I know…"

Audience #1: "I have a three year old – you want to change that!"

Catalano: "Hi Freddie…"

Audience #1: "God damn it!"

Catalano: "I'm sorry, look… I know I smell of perfume but it's not what you think. I was… you didn't know that did you?"

Audience #2: "Freeze!"

Audience #1: You… (Crying)

(Audience laughter. Then a new audience member enters and creates and entirely new scene. Catalano exits improvisation.)

Catalano: Thank you… perfect…

(Audience #1 is female and Audience #2 is male.)

Audience #2:	The aircraft looked like this... it rolled, it came on full throttle and I fired a missile down on it... it missed. It went for a roll down here... and what should I have done next?
Audience #1:	"Then what the fuck were you doing over in Israel?"
	(Audience laughter)
Audience #2:	"I was fighting Arabs what else do you think I was doing over Israel?"
Audience #1:	"Did you not see the sign on the plane? It was not the Arabs you hit!"
Audience #2:	"I wasn't..."
Catalano:	"Freeze..."

Excellent... excellent. I don't know if you noticed what he did? He took the physical space exactly and he made it into something else. That normally takes a long time for people to get and he just got it right out of the box. That's exactly right. Let's continue.

(Improvisation begins. Audience #1 and Audience #2 are both female.)

Audience #1:	(crying) "You told me you wouldn't tell them... you lied..."
Audience #2:	"I'm sorry... but you know I had to... it was my job. I'm a counselor and I had to tell the authorities."
Audience #1:	"Now, they're going to lock me up... (crying.)

Audience #2:   "They won't… they'll just give you counseling."

Audience #1:   (more crying)

Catalano: "Freeze…"

(Catalano tags out one person and brings in another member of the audience.)

Catalano: "Anyone you want…"

Audience #1:   "I'll take her."

Catalano: "Excellent work."

(Audience #1 is male and Audience #2 is female.)

Audience #1:   "So, when I talked to Miss Suliman, I said that I thought it was actually nine embryos not just eight. So I don't know what happened. So, what am I supposed to tell the press?"

Audience #2:   "Well, first of all… you need to learn how to count. This very important Yuk Yuk Yuk – how did you pass medical school?"

Audience #1:   "Well, this wasn't my first language. You know this… I don't know what I'm going do though because the press is hounding me for more and more information and they think that I'm a creep because I put all these embryos in there…"

(Catalano cuts in.)

Catalano: "Freeze…"

(Brings in a new audience member to tag someone out.)

Catalano: "Anyone you want."

(A new improvisation is started Audience #1 is a male and Audience #2 is a female.)

Audience #1: "What did you expect I would think when you come in wearing…fishnet hose and a short skirt?"

Audience #2: "I'm sorry honey, I didn't think you would notice. Didn't you realize where the extra money was coming from? It's not my fault! You know! I mean I'm paying for all your fancy cars – I had to get the money somewhere.

Audience #1: "I'm not complaining about the money or even where it came from… but you didn't tell me. I can't pass on it… the right amount of funds to our agent – he has to know where our source of supply comes from otherwise he might complain about the wrong ten percent.

Audience #2: "You can't tell him… you can't tell him… tell him that I'm working on the wrong side of the street!"

(Catalano ends the improvisation.)

Catalano: "…and freeze."

Good, let's make a circle… will you join us?

(Audience member reluctantly joins the group.)

(Audience laughter.)

13

You Don't Have To Be Funny to Improvise

Writing on your Feet

Now there's something I want to say about improvisation, I don't really need to say it here, but sometimes people participating, tell me if you think it's true, that they feel they have to be funny when they come up here. What you do and say always has to be funny?

(Several audience members indicate agreement.)

Well, it doesn't. So, you can have some real moments up here... not everything is a Saturday Night Live skit... we can also do drama. We will be doing some longer form sitting down in a minute. Now, I want to just try something – it doesn't have to be funny – it can be just real. Especially, if you are working on a dramatic piece. But dramatic pieces can also have humor in them too.

How many of you had difficulty coming up with the first line when you entered the improvisations today?

(Many of the audience members raise their hands in agreement.)

Okay, I'm going to fix that right now. I want everyone to think of a first line and make it so that it is something you can remember.

(Catalano welcomes the new member of the audience who has finally stepped into the group.)

By the way, I'm Frank Catalano.

(Audience member: "I'm Maggie.)

Hi Maggie.	How do you do? Okay, here we go… okay, so what's your first line?
Audience:	"What are you doing here?"
Audience:	"Why did you kill my child?"
Audience:	"But I always wanted to do that."
Audience:	"Hello, Frankie angel…"
Audience:	"I don't want to do much of anything."

Okay, that's a good start… should I have a first line too? Here's mine

Catalano:	"I'll take cherry vanilla."

I hope I don't forget that… I know I will.

Alright, let's spread out a bit and let's start with two people in the center and we will start the first line of the improvisation with the line you have selected and the person already in the circle will respond with their first line Every time someone is tagged out, the new person coming in will always start (no matter what the physicality of the position they are taking) with the line they have selected. You know the ones we said when we went around the circle a moment ago.

Let's give a try:

>(Two audience members take the center of the circle and begin)

>(Note they will always be identified as Audience #1 and Audience #2.)

Audience #1: "Hello, Frankie Angel..."

Audience #2: "What are you doing here?"

Audience #1: "Well, just... oh wait you weren't Frankie Angel. I'm so sorry, my bad... well I guess I better go now."

Audience #2: "You obviously don't know what the hell you're doing here?"

Audience #1: "Well... actually I don't. You know... Well my "meds" I thought I was going to be on certain "meds" and they got them mixed up and now I'm... I think I'm lost."

Audience #2: "You're lost? I've got some "meds" here if you need them."

Okay cut. Good.

>(One audience member remains and one steps out of the center of the circle and is replaced by a different audience member.)

Come on in... remember you start with your first line and you respond with your first line.

Audience #1: (whisper) Why did you kill my child?"

Audience #2: "Hello, Frankie Angel..."

Audience #1: "You're caught..."

Audience #2: "I'm who?"

Audience #1: "You're caught... I died to come after you."

Audience #2: "What?"

Audience #1: "I want to know **why** you killed my child."

Audience #2: "I don't think I know... oh my goodness, that was your child? I thought that was my child. I'm confused, that was your child?"

Audience #1: "I gave birth to him..."

Audience #2: "Wait... that was **our** child... why are you saying it's your child. It's always about your child... it's always about your needs. What about **my** needs?

Audience #1: "I gave birth to him... I have the sagging breasts... I have the cesarean scar to prove it!"

Audience #2: "You know what? Prove it!"

And cut... that was good. That was great!

(Audience laughter)

Should we write that down? That was good. Oaky, let's go back out... are you okay with this?

(Audience member responds with a "yes."

I thought you said you didn't like improvisation. You know what this is... she's a "plant" who knows how to do this cold. She is going to just come in

(Audience laughter.)

and says to herself "I'm just going to play this fool..." Okay, you have your first line. Let's do another one.

Audience #1:	"I never want to do much of anything."	
Audience #2:	"But I always wanted to do this..."	
Audience #1:	"But I don't..."	
Audience #2:	"But I do... and I thought..."	
Audience #1:	"Oh, please..."	
Audience #2:	"But it's really fun... it's really fun... it's great... it's great."	
Audience #1:	"It could be..."	
Audience #2:	"...and that parachute on the back... ignore the bricks... they put bricks in the special back packs. But's it's okay; you're going to love this. They're going to put you in a plane. It will be fabulous – you signed the insurance policy. Right?"	

Audience #1:	"Sure… whatever. Just somebody is going to have to push me… because I'm not going otherwise."
Audience #2:	"They'll push you… they'll push you. I'll push you."

And cut. Good… very Hitchcock…

(Audience laughter.)

Let's bring in a new person and a new line.

(Audience member leaves and a different one enters the circle.)

You start.

Audience #1:	"I don't want to do much of anything."
Audience #2:	"What are you doing here?"
Audience #1:	"I just walked in by mistake and it was a mistake but I didn't realize you guys would ask me to do anything."

(Audience laughter)

Audience #2:	"You mean you walked through a door that says "ACTION IN HERE" and you expected no action?
Audience #1:	"It didn't say that. It didn't say anything like that."
Audience #2:	"Did you read the door?"
Audience #1:	"No…"

Audience #2: "Oh come on... it's on the door – I wrote it there..."

Audience #1: "You did?"

Audience #2: "Yes, I wrote there... I took my pen and I wrote it there."

And cut... good! Don't run away.

(Audience laughter.)

Okay, who do I want to pair up? Okay... you start.

Audience #1: "What are you doing here?"

Catalano: "I'd like a cherry vanilla..."

Audience #1: "A cherry vanilla?"

Catalano: "Yes, sir."

Audience #1: "I'm sorry, we don't have cherry vanilla."

Catalano: "Oh? I saw cherry over there and vanilla over here and I thought maybe you could put them together."

Audience #1: "If you saw an elephant over there and a zebra over there would you put them together?"

Catalano: "Look, my kid's in the car... can you give me a break? He's crying and the kid gives me... you know I really shouldn't even be here. I took..."

Audience #1: "Look, all I have here Pee Boo Bear and Black Walnut... would you like a shake?"

Catalano:	"No, you know I took my kid… I'm not supposed to have him. My wife doesn't even know I have him and he's very upset… if you could just help me out."
Audience #1:	"Okay… is he allergic to nuts?"
Catalano:	"You know, I don't know… just give me a little cherry… I tell you what… give me two cones… one cherry and one vanilla and I'll put them together myself. Okay?"
Audience #1:	"All right, I've got some cherry here… and how about a vanilla bean?"
Catalano:	"Great… how much is that… here… I'll give you twenty bucks."
Audience #1:	"Twenty bucks… sure!"
Catalano:	"Thanks a lot."
Audience #1:	"Sure you don't want any walnut?"
Catalano:	"No, listen I gotta go… I gotta go."

Improvisation ends.

And so on… what you can see is, that you can have comedy, you can make what is said into something else. You don't have to be literal. The "Hello Frankie Angel" line does not always have to be comic. It also depends on what is added to by the other actor. You can use dialogue totally against the literal meaning or character. You can give them any meaning you want them to have within the reality of the scene. There could be an assassin and this character could be a stand up comedian. I mean it could be that kind of a thing. It doesn't always have to be literal. It's not like playing the piano where the dark lower notes are here and the higher notes are here... you can mix these elements to create your characters and story. You have to remain open and let the improvisation take you to wherever it takes you. Okay, let's try something else. Let's all sit down... you can rest now. And what I would like to do is create a scenario... without being literal.

14

FINDING THE METAPHOR – HOW *NOT* TO BE LITERAL

Writing on your Feet

OKAY. I WANT to create a scenario where there is nothing and try one or two with an actual framework given… like a break up or something like that where you can actually work within a narrative framework. But I want to try this exercise first because it will be fun… and you can sit down on this one, which will be great. Right?

(Audience laughter.)

This is not a "tag" scene and I will need two volunteers. Great! Thank you.

(Catalano pulls two people from the audience.)

(Audience laughter)

You are so kind. Great. Frankie Angel, I knew I could count on you. That's such a great opening line. Please come and sit down. So what we are trying to do here, if we may, and again what we are about to do is a "conceit" a bit of a trick. Let's say you are sitting in front of a blank page and you have absolutely "zip." What if we just had two characters, just like the two people sitting here today… and we have nothing but a blank page? What I want to do is start with a single word which one of you sitting here will say and one of you in the audience will give me in a minute. The word we start with will be a random word that the audience will give us.

Now before we begin, let me remind you (we are kind of there already) that whatever the word is, we do not have to stick to the literal meaning of that word. The word could mean something else entirely. For example, if we started with the word "brick," the entire scene would not have to be about construction materials. A "brick" could mean anything… what are some things a brick could mean?

(Audience members speak.)

"Something heavy."
"Bulky"
"A person's name."
"A blockage of some sort."
"A part of something."

All possible. So I don't want you to get tied into being literal. Use your imagination and see where the word you start with takes you and remember, don't go crazy trying to think of something funny. Just be in the moment. So, if we start with a word like "anchovies" the scene doesn't have to be about fish. The word could mean anything… it could act as a metaphor for your life. So, you can take it to another level or in some cases you might want to use the literal.

(Audience member: "How you hear it.")

How you hear it... the way it is spoken... the context it is given within a scene. Now for our exercise, we are going to start you with a single word. All I want you to do is say that word and you will respond. Don't add any other word to what you say. Don't say, "Anchovies, I hate that restaurant." Just start with the word and don't try to define it. Let it define itself through the exchange of dialogue. Allow your partner to hear the word and then respond and then you respond to that line and so forth. The meaning and direction of the scene will happen on its own. It's a give and take kind of a feel. Now, I'm not going to let this scene go on forever, just a couple of lines to see what emerges out of it. Okay? Ready? Go...

Audience #1: "Cumquat."

Audience #2: "Would you please?"

Audience #1: "Isn't this a nice restaurant."

Audience #2: "(laughter) This is our third date."

Audience #1: "You know, the funny thing about that is... I wasn't sure there would be a third date... and I figured, well if there's going to be a third date I'm just going to be who I am.

(Audience #2 gives Audience #1 a strange look)

(Audience laughter.)

Audience #2: "Do you know that I could have been out with this other guy. But I thought you were nice. My mother recommended you."

Audience #1: "Well, I never actually got to the third date with your mother. But..."

Audience #2: (Gasp)

(Audience laughter.)

Audience #1: "The cumquats she gave me in appreciation for the last time we were out... were sort of appropriate."

Audience #2: "My mother has lived with my father for forty years. You screwed my mother."

Audience #1: "Oh no... I got as far with her as I am with you right now."

(Audience laughter.)

"Now, I have more cumquats back at my place."

(Audience laughter)

And cut. Let's talk about this. We started with cumquat – a very simple concept and it became this whole thing about infidelity. The challenge here is to go beyond the word cumquat. I mean the literal word and make it take you to somewhere else. I think both of you did a great job listening to one another. That is an important element that must be present if the creative arc is to be achieved. Sometimes in improvisation, the people working don't listen to one another. Instead, they just try to push through their own idea for the scene no matter what the other person is doing or saying. It makes it very difficult for the scene to progress when this happens. You want your improvisation, not matter how it starts, to be engaging to the participants and the audience alike. Now let's have two more volunteers.

(Two new but reluctant audience members come up on the stage.)

Come on, you can do this.

(A totally new person enters the room and comes up upon the stage.)

Okay, I'm going to set you up on this because you are coming in cold. We are going to give you a line – one of the audience members is going to give you a line. This gentleman here has volunteered to give you a line.

(Audience laughter.)

Now we want to give you a whole line (not just a word). So, think of something good. We will do two of these. The first, we will start with just one line and we will see what evolves. You may get up and move around if you want. Now for the audience here, let's bring it back home to where we started. We are writing and we have nothing more than a blank page in front of us.

(Catalano is given the ten-minute signal.)

Ten minutes? Great. The first time we did this we put the word cumquat on a blank page, then we added to characters and we watched what evolved. Now, we are still on a blank page, we have two characters and in a moment one line. But we are not providing any of who, what, when or where. Visualize what is about to happen as a single line on a blank page. And now the line is?

Audience member: "I thought my turrets was cured."

(Audience member on stage looking out at the suggested first line says "I'm going to kill you for this.")

(Audience laughter.)

Audience #1: "I thought my turrets was cured."

Audience #2: "I did too… but it sure isn't."

Audience #1: "No, it isn't."

Audience #2: "I guess you're mad."

Audience #1: "I am… it comes out all the time."

Audience #2: "You're really an embarrassment to the family."

Audience #1: "Oh, well? I can handle that.

Audience #2: "Why don't you get a handle on it?

Audience #1: "It's just…"

Audience #2: "No, it's weakness. You're just a weak person.

Audience #1: "Well, it's really…"

Audience #2: "You're just an embarrassment to the whole family. We are all successful and you sit around with this… this"

Audience #1: "Well…"

Audience #2: "It's not that… It's just like this, fuck, shit damn get out of my face.

Audience #1 "I can imagine that it would be an embarrassment to everybody, but I kind of like that."

Audience #2: "You like it? You like embarrassing all of us? We all have doctorates and masters and you're going to embarrass the family."

Audience #1: "Well, I have a doctorate but…"

Audience #2: "Then why don't you go live in a cabin somewhere in the woods?"

Audience #1: "Well, I'm looking for one."

Audience #2: "Well, I hope you find one."

Audience #1: "Okay, I will."

Audience #2: "If you'll just go live there and stay away from the rest of the family and quit embarrassing us."

Audience #1: "Okay."

Audience #2: "Okay."

Okay, cut.

(Audience laughter.)

Okay, think of a line.

(Audience member "Did that improvisation have to be so mean?)

No, but it kind of went that way. But did you notice that the characters had a particular physicality and sound to them? Now for this next exercise we're going to think of a line and we're going to end it in that line. Let's call it "Last Line." We are just going to start cold and develop the "who, what, when and where," but as the scene progresses at some point (when it reaches a natural climax) we will end it with this line. The scene is not over until the last line is spoken within the context of the scene.

(Audience member asks: "Are we continuing the turrets scene?")

No, this is a totally new scene where we will create a totally new who, what, when and where. What I would like you to work on and think about is who you are and what is happening. Then as the scene comes to a natural conclusion, you will end it with this last line. We know it's over when the last line is spoken. So, if the last line given were "Merry Christmas," the improvisation is not over until that line is spoken.

(Audience member: "Does it matter who says the line?")

No.

(Audience member: "So it's over whenever that line is spoken?")

Right.

(Audience member: "So, how do you get started?")

You just start with in this instance two characters in the room. Let me help you out a little bit. You're sitting in a waiting room for a job interview and the last line is? "So why is the lowest grade you got in ballroom dance?"

Audience #1: "What are you waiting for?"

Audience #2: "I'm interviewing for a part time position as an editor."

Audience #1: "Oh, I'm interviewing for the full time as an editor."

Audience #2: "Well, good. Then we're on different tracks."

Audience #1: "I think there's only one position though…"

Audience #2: "Do you think they made a mistake. I mean part time? Full time? You know?"

Audience #1: "As far as I know there is only one position and if they can get somebody to work full time with part time pay."

(Audience laughter.)

Audience #1: "They would rather have them… than a part time."

Audience #2: "Well, we will just have to see. How did you get into this business?"

Audience #1: "Went to school… then just did some writing… then some editing. What about you?"

Audience #2: "Well, I just need some money. So I do whatever I can. I hope it's part time – I really don't want to work full time. Well, we will just have to see. But… what else to do you do?"

Audience #1: "Well actually… I don't work at all. In fact, I just came into this room by accident. I'm a student.

Audience #2: "College?"

Audience #1: "You're probably thinking I'm way to old to go to college… but actually, I do very well. I have almost a 4.0 GPA."

Audience #2: "Really? Why almost?"

> Audience #1: Well, all can't be good at everything. I got a "D" in ballroom dance…"
>
> Audience #2: "So why is the lowest grade you got in ballroom dance?"

And cut. Tune in next week to find out "why" her lowest grade was in ballroom dance. Perhaps she was doing a bit more than ballroom dancing with her partner Renaldo!"

Out of this scene, maybe two characters would evolve. Maybe they would become friends, leave the job interview go on an adventure. Maybe they decide to rob a bank or go on a spree… two women meet and want to change their boring lives. What do we have *Thelma and Louise (1991)*. And it all starts with two people meeting at a job interview and from that point the characters and the story evolve. Remember we started with a blank page and now we have three pages of dialogue. We may use very little of it or all of it… but we have now progressed off of the blank page to an idea. An idea that will evolve on it's own rather than be artificially crafted. We now have the beginning of our story and we have begun our journey on our feet!

I want to thank all of you for getting up here on this stage today. Let's all give one another a big round of applause for doing such a great job today!

Thank you very much and I hope you enjoy the rest of the conference. Thank you.

(Audience applause.)

START YOUR STORY AT THE END

SAN DIEGO STATE UNIVERSITY
25th Annual Writers Conference

HOW TO ADAPT YOUR NOVEL INTO A SCREENPLAY

BOOK 3

Frank Catalano

15

What I Learned Working at a Motion Picture Studio

Start Your Story at the End

It's been a great opportunity for me to have been able to spend time working at both motion picture studios and academia. You learn a lot when working at a motion picture studio. How films and made and more importantly how films are marketed to the public. One of the things I learned very early on is that motion picture companies are creative places to work, but they are also businesses that have to make a profit. Very much like an automobile company or any factory has to make money on what they sell.

It reminds me of the famous Garson Kanin quote about making movies:

"So it can be seen that the trouble with the motion-picture art was (and is) that it is too much an industry; and the trouble with the motion picture industry is that it is too much an art. It is out of this basic contradiction that most of the ills of the form arise."

So while, you may have the most wonderfully written novel or screenplay in your back pocket that you are trying to get produced, inevitably questions are going to be asked like who is directing and who is the star? They will want to know: "Who is attached to it?" What does that mean? It means what marketable entity (actor, writer, producer) is attached to your project that will ensure its success at the box office. We all like to see recognizable names attached to what we see in the movies. Why, because it gives us an idea of what we can expect to see. So, if the name Brad Pitt is above the title as actor, or Steven Spielberg as director, we will have a certain expectation of what we will experience. The creation of motion pictures and television is an art but it is equally a business. Working at a movie studio taught me a lot about that. But really, this idea of attachments is really another topic.

Someone should do a seminar entitled HOW TO GET BRAD PIT IN YOUR MOVIE.

(Audience laughter)

Once, you have that level of attachment, the doors start to open. And, if I might say, that has nothing to do with the writing – which is why we are here today.

The second thing I learned, really very early on is "no matter how wonderful your idea is…" And I'm sure you all have intriguing subjects and characters in your work. But, no matter how wonderful your idea is, they will want to know if your work will able to appeal to a segment of the market. Any many many times, you will get these two criticisms of your work – "You have a wonderful idea… but it doesn't fit the market we are trying to reach." The second criticism or negative statement is perhaps your work is too much like one they already have in the pipeline. So you are stopped cold right at the start. I haven't even mentioned the word script, but you may not even get that far… your script could be in your back pocket. They will say you have a wonderful idea but it will not do very well in the particular market in which they produce or they may view your creation to be marketed to a specific market segment. You may believe, as you sit here this morning, that a film or book for that matter should just be "general" so that the highest number of audience will buy it. But it doesn't work that way. It's the exact opposite. We, all of us, are broken down into demographic groupings and separated by gender, age, income, where we live and educational levels. So if your idea is general, they may not know where or how to market it. Please remember, that this has absolutely nothing to do with the quality of your writing or idea. You may have a wonderful story that you feel needs to be told, but in todays' marketplace it is not enough. There needs to be a correlation to what you have written directly to a specific market or it must have a well known talent attached to it. That well known talent will provide a producer with a measurable way to estimate how your script will do if it is produced.

However, most of you are fiction writers, so you may have works already published. In this instance a producer can look at the markets you have reached with your book and get an idea how it might do as a film or television production. But if you are going in with just a story that you feel needs to be told… they won't really give this type of criteria much consideration. You could have proof (detailed images) of an extra terrestrial landing in a spaceship and proof that there is life in other worlds. As earth shattering as that may seem, they may still pass on your script if they can't figure out how to sell it. They will be thinking, right now, in this market at this time how would this project do? And to this day, I have a hard time getting wrapped around that way of thinking. I can understand it from a financial perspective; but as a creative person, I just don't understand it.

When I first went to work at Warner Brother studios, I was so excited to be part of a landmark studio where such great films had been made. I was working at the smaller Lorimar Studio that primarily produced television programming such as *Dallas (1978-1991), Knots Landing (1979 – 1993) and Full House (1987 – 1995)*. Warner Brothers eventually bought Lorimar and so after that I went to Warner Brothers. When I first got on the Warner Brother lot, I was a like a child at a candy store. I walked past the very same sound stages where many classic films were made; *The Maltese Falcon (1941), Casablanca (1942), The Big Sleep (1946)* and where great stars like Betty Davis, Errol Flynn, or Humphrey Bogart created unforgettable characters. This in my mind was a very special place but I learned very quickly, that the Warner

Brothers I was thinking of was no longer in existence. The studio was part of a larger corporate entity AOL Time Warner and later after they sold off AOL – they became Time Warner. Warner Brothers was no longer a studio that just made movies, it was a corporate powerhouse creating entertainment for a multitude of media and outlets. It didn't matter to them what they were creating. It just happened to be entertainment programming. However, it could have just as easily been electronic devices, computers or automobiles. They were a full-fledged business focused on the bottom line. Now let's not wax nostalgic for the old studio days when the four Warner Brothers ran the company. It was a business then as well, focused on creating and releasing movies (as many as one per week) to fill company owned movie theatres around the world. They were a business, just like Ford Motor Company or GM. However, they, like every other studio head, created movies for their particular audience. Yes, they were companies and this did manufacture product, it was the same as rolling a car off the assembly line. Today, the environment is very different.

16

Adapting your Novel into a Screenplay

Start Your Story at the End

When writers and other creative people interact with the motion picture business culture, they often do so at a disadvantage. They are under the assumption that a great idea or well-written script is what they will need when they walk in the door. Of course, everyone wants the work they do to be of the best quality and creativity. However, the real driving factor for any studio executive at some point in the process will be to get a handle on whether the idea or the script has a market. Will anyone want to experience in any form, what you have written? The answer should be "Yes…" but you should also know "why." Now I have a quick question for all of you. How many of you are active screenwriters. I ask this because, I know this is a conference of fiction and non-fiction writers. How many of you have screenplays that you have written?

(Several audience members raise their hands)

How many of you have completed novels?

(A larger segment of the audience raises their hands)

Okay, great! How many of you are thinking about converting your existing novel into a screenplay?

(A large portion of the audience raises their hands)

Excellent. I think it's a great thing to do. If you sell your book and that sale includes screen rights, it's always nice to have it available as part of your package. If you have representation they will look upon it as a positive thing. However, it is not a guarantee that you will be able to write the screenplay version of your own book. Producers, more often than not, will buy the movie rights for a particular work and then assign their own screenwriter to develop it for film. Often, even then, the screenplay is often written by a series of screenwriters developing a series of drafts toward the completed version. Each producer likes to have writers that they have worked with before create the script versions of their films. Why? They might like a particular writer for his or her style or the success of their previous scripts at the box office. I am telling you this now up front so that you know that your book may be purchased for screen and you may have a fully written screenplay that will not be considered. You might even be paid for it but it might never be drawn upon and you would not receive any screen credit. It's the nature of the way things are done in the film business. So you may be thinking, "If my screenplay is probably not going to be used, why am I sitting here today in this seminar START YOUR STORY AT THE END?" What's the idea behind the title START YOUR STORY AT THE END?

Why would you want to invest time into writing a screenplay? Why are we really here today? When you saw the title START YOUR STORY AT THE END, what did you think it really meant?

(Audience member raises their hand)

Yes?

(Audience member: "When I am working on the story for my book, I kept visualizing it thinking this would be great on the screen – I kind of though you were talking about that as you write the original novel you would visualize your story for the screen.)

Okay. In a way I am. If you are currently working on a novel, it's always a great idea to visualize how it would look up on the screen. Are the visual images I am creating for my book compelling and would they pull an audience into my story? Or am I writing talking heads, just kind of sitting in one spot for an extended period of time having a conversation? Which is it? I am not suggesting that your characters have to be in a constant state of motion, they can talk, they can stand still, they can relate to one another in a non-physical way. All of these things are possible. However, never forget that film and television are visual mediums that convey their story be showing as well as telling. But there's a larger framework. I want you to all think about something. We are all consumers and when we are asked to invest or buy something, we are very careful of how we spend our time and money. We check everything out on the Internet because we can. We all want to be sure about the outcome of everything we do.

I just attended the opening night of a wonderful new play called Minsky's that just bowed at the Ahmanson Theatre in Los Angeles and then plans to continue on to Broadway. Now the story of Minsky's is not a new idea. It was made into a film in in *1968 – The Night They Raided Minsky's* that was a fictional account about the invention of striptease at a burlesque house in turn of the century New York City. The new musical comedy MINSKY'S takes all that into account and adds of course great music, a love story and very creative choreography. But this is a new treatment of the idea and audiences want to know right away (in advance if we can give it to them) if they buy tickets to this show it will be money well spent. What am I hinting at? We all want to know the future when we invest our time and money into something. We want to know how it will all turn out. We want to know as soon as possible and if we can't get the future up front, we want to have an indication of how it will be pretty early on. We are an "immediate gratification" society that needs to be pulled in quickly or we will lose interest... move on to the next thing. Okay, now back to writing.

In your screenplay, no matter what, you have got to connect to your audience right away... I'd say the first ten pages or the first ten minutes of your movie. You don't have to tell the whole story, but you have got that much space and time to get your audience connected and on board. If you do what I call a "slow roll out" of your story and characters, then you run the risk of losing your audience because they are not connected to your characters or story. So, you're thinking to your self "okay, that's it... start my story at the end, then they'll be hooked. But wait, if I'm at the end, it's over... I'll have nothing else to tell." No. Maybe the title is misleading and should be called START YOUR STORY "ALMOST" AT THE END.

(Audience laughter)

You want to begin at a pivotal moment at the end of your story. Show them your central characters if you can put them in peril. But don't give it all away.... Just give the reader enough to wonder about what they are see, what they are hear and ponder what will happen next. The will instantaneously want to know how it will all turn out... and you will be happy to take them there. But first they must go back to the beginning and find out what has lead them to that pivotal moment. In short, they will have to read the whole screenplay to find out. But this is something you can't force someone to do... they have to want to read it. They have to be compelled to do it. It is the same reason; drivers always slow down as they pass a traffic accident. They want to know, as best they can, what has happened and as they drive by and get a sense of how it will all turn out in the end. Modern audiences want some sort of assurance that any investment made in either time or money will have a return. This is one part of it.

17

Write Like You're Buying Toothpaste

Start Your Story at the End

THE OTHER PART of it is, when we buy something... let's say when we buy toothpaste... you're thinking right now, I thought we were talking about writing. Now we are talking about buying toothpaste? Trust me this all will tie in. When you buy toothpaste, do you think about the process of using the toothpaste or do you think about the end. Now all toothpaste cleans your teeth. But why do we buy a certain brand?

(Audience member: "Because it fights cavities.")

Right. But doesn't all toothpaste do that. Is there something else?

(Audience member: "Makes our teeth clean?")

Right. Anything else?

(Audience member: "Price?")

Okay, so you buy one brand over another because it costs less. Right? But it still does the same things... I mean, clean your teeth, fight cavities... all of that?

(Audience: "Makes your teeth whiter?")

Yes, now we're getting somewhere. How do you know that it does all these things? How do we know it makes our teeth whiter, or brighter?

(Audience: "It's on the package and in advertising.")

Right. And that is a promise made to you. If you buy this toothpaste, it will make your teeth brighter or whiter. All advertising does this. It makes a promise to us; if you invest your time and money in this product it will do something in return. This is a promise. Now let's go back to writing and your original idea.

Let's go back to that very moment when you had the original idea for the book you have written or the book you will write. It was or is an idea and you thought about writing a story that you felt needed to be told. But step away from that and put yourself in the reader's seat and ask this question.

"What is the promise you are making to your reader?"

Essentially, can you make this promise – if you read my book or screenplay I promise that you will experience a Non-stop suspense thriller, a knee slapping comedy or a tender love story. It can't be all of these these things, but it should be a least one idea that an audience can identify with. It's just like buying that tube of toothpaste, there needs to be a singular overriding reason that we want it and then buy it. The process is exactly the same in writing.

Think about what you have written. Can you answer this question? Can you tell anyone or me who might ask in one sentence the type of story you have written? We all go home and slug away on our laptops and struggle to tell our story. When it's done, we can sit back and feel a sense of accomplishment. It's done. But can you look someone in the eye, and say read this book... read this screenplay and if you do, I promise that it will be this our that. You fill in the blank.... and whatever it is you choose to say, make it compelling. Make it sound like something they will have to read because if they don't, they will miss out. To quote the Godfather, "make them an offer they can't refuse."

(Audience laughter)

Perhaps some of you can ask the question, but as yet don't have an answer.

The answer is everything... and if you have the answer and it is clear as day, you think to yourself that this is it, I have something. So this is the second point, make a promise to your audience. In order to do that, you have got to have a clear understanding of what your story is and more importantly how it will fit in and be perceived by an audience. So let's summarize.

1. You begin your story at a pivotal moment in the plot at the end of the story. A point that there is no return and you show your central character – hopefully in some sort of peril.
2. Once you take your audience to the pivotal moment, make them a promise. If you read this book or screenplay, I promise you this outcome.

This takes us right back to buying toothpaste. If you pull your audience in at a pivotal moment then make them a promise of how it will all be and it you fulfill it – they will be happy. Just like buying toothpaste that promises to make your teeth whiter. If you buy it, and your teeth are whiter you are happy. At that point, the toothpaste is no longer toothpaste. It has become an enabler improving your understanding of life and happiness in so many ways. Am I saying that your adapted screenplay must change the lives (become an enabler) for all those who experience it? Isn't a good story and well developed characters enough? No, I don't think so. I think your writing needs to go beyond just a story and characters. We are bombarded every day with images, and stories and characters in all parts of our life. Our brain filters most of these stimuli out and only focuses on those things that somehow within our presentation connect to our audience in an intellectual, emotional, physical or spiritual way. Everything else is just noise.

18

Presenting Your Story to an Audience

Start Your Story at the End

Let's look at four elements briefly. What do I actually mean when I say present your story to your reader (audience) intellectually, emotionally, physically or spiritually? You don't have to achieve all four. However, your work should make a connection on a least one of these levels.

Intellectual:
Your story and characters present an idea that a reader or audience can clearly understand and connect with on an intellectual level. Most murder mysteries or thrillers connect to an audience this way. Think about scripts like *The Usual Suspects (1995), The Butterfly Effect (2004) or Inception (2010), Gone Girl (2014)*.

Emotional:
Your story and characters evoke certain emotions in the reader or audience. Think about scripts like *the Notebook (2004), Schindler's List (1993)* or *The Boy in the Striped Pajamas (2008)*.

Physical:
Your story and characters cause the reader or audience member to react physically. This can be something they do afterwards or it can change their physical behavior. Think about movies such as *Rocky Horror Picture Show (1975), Rocky IV (1985), Erin Brockovich (2000)* and *Jaws (1975) and Jurassic World (2015).*

Spiritual:
Your story and characters connect to the value system of the reader that benefits their souls and connects them consciously or perhaps even unconsciously with their own existence within the universe. Think about scripts and films like *Gandhi (1982), Castaway (2000)* or *The Life of Pi (2012).*

So let's look at the ways we use to present our stories and characters. We can look at this presentation in terms of three formats:

The Pitch:

A pitch meeting usually takes place in an office setting where you will present your idea (not script) to one or more persons. Now, I want to stop here and say that a pitch meeting on its face value is of course talking about your idea. But it is not as simple as that. When you into such a meeting it is important to build a connection with this person, perhaps establishing a connection by mentioning someone you both know. This will sound strange, but I think it's important to let them do the talking. Let them tell you about themselves, the kind of projects they do and what they are looking for. This will make them feel better about themselves and like you for allowing them to do it. Finally, when your moment arrives to talk about your idea, make sure it is prepared. Don't just make it up as you go. You should have a rehearsed set of bullet points when you present your idea. Be prepared and start your story at the end and make them want to wonder how it will all turn out in the end. If they have any questions or criticisms, try to address them but don't get defensive. Lastly, close them. Just like they do, you want to know what's going to happen next and get them to give you an indication of what that will be.

The pitch then, is a very short form way to present your story. But all the same concepts we have discussed here should apply.

The Treatment – a summary of your script or book

A treatment is often referred to as a blue print for a full script just as a screenplay is the blue print for the full movie. In this shortened version or preview you need to state your idea, its story, characters and somehow frame it in a way that they will love it so much that they will want to read the whole script. I will be honest with you. I hate the idea of a treatment. I'd rather do a pitch and then go directly to script. A treatment is like eating part of a meal. When you serve it, you have little or no control over whether they will like those parts you are serving. I'm having the Tuscan Chicken this evening only I am have a small bite with two carrots and a sliver of potato. I hate dark meat.

(Audience laughter)

The truth is, the Tuscan Chicken has both and also other vegetables but I only was served the carrots. It's a losing proposition. I'd rather pitch the idea and make them want to read the whole script or in reality have someone else read the whole script. I think treatments are fine, if you want to use it for your own internal purposes to see how your book will translate into the film medium.

Coverage – the script itself

Producers receive massive amounts of material both in screenplay and book formats. In order to meet this demand, they often have submitted material covered by a reader. Readers will review the material and prepare a three or four page report called coverage. Their coverage usually summarizes the plot, characters, estimated budget and offers an opinion as to whether or not the script is a good fit for their company. In this scenario, you are submitting your material to a second person, perhaps one you haven't even met, who will determine if your project will go on to the next level. Here more than ever, it is important to open your story at the end and create a sense of tension that will make the reader want to find out what happens.

You are probably thinking, what about the story. Isn't a good story the most important thing to consider? We all have been taught the linear story from kindergarten forward. The classic fairy tale stories that begin with "once upon a time…" So we have all become accustomed to the narrative going from "A" to "B" to "C." However, having someone tell a child a fairy tale with all the appropriate plot structure is quite different than trying to tell you story to a reader. You don't have the time, to tell the whole story with a little bit of exposition shared along the way and then it all ends with the traditional climax and resolution. You have got to get them up front or risk losing them forever.

Perhaps technology has made us all somewhat impatient – when we want to know something we just look it up on the Internet. We speak a command into our hand held device and the answer is delivered to us within seconds. When it doesn't come to us right away, we just move on to something else. Most of the time, we are concerned with the end result, not the process of how we got there. And isn't that often what good writing is, it is a process of discovery through the use of language. You write a great story with wonderful characters and you want people to read it. Yes?

(Audience nods in agreement)

However, because it is presented in this sort of heightened artificial state, those elements that are normally considered part of great writing are put in the back seat. I often wonder, if any of Shakespeare's plays receiving coverage today would ever be fully read or moved on to production? I can see it now, Romeo and Juliet "nice dialogue but needs to get to the point more quickly. Plot too complicated – recommend cutting the Friar and apothecary and combine them with other characters.""

(Audience laughter)

Something like that…

19

EVERYONE IS CONCERNED WITH THE END RESULT NOT THE PROCESS

Start Your Story at the End

EVERYONE IS CONCERNED with end result and not the process of how we get there. You are sitting here and thinking, I want to show my characters – how they go through a process of self-discovery and finally at the end… they discover the true meaning to life. It' is very exhilarating! The problem is, while it may be a wonderful story and the characters may be compelling to read as they go through their journey of self-discovery, no one will ever know. Why? Because they won't read it and so it will not be made. So, do we all turn into mindless automatons and write artificial senseless dribble so they will read it? You're thinking… isn't that most television?

(Audience laughter)

No, we stay true to our stories and our characters but we just present them within this heightened form a bit differently. We could take *Gone With the Wind (1939)* and write a pitch for it so that it would get read. Incidentally, *Gone with the Wind* would be an extremely difficult pitch today. Why? It is a larger than life, epic that is a period picture that would have to be done with mega stars so that it could generate the box office to pay for itself. I can see the producer's coverage now-– "very expensive, we would have to burn Atlanta, and have several large battle scenes –recommend changing to current period making it a modern thriller, alien invaders on the city of Washington and Brad Pitt to play Rhett Butler."

(Audience laughter)

All right? One other thing I will mention is run time. When you write your books, you may take as many pages as you like to develop your characters and story. You will have to make choices in film. Think about your expectation when watching a movie in a theatre. How long do you anticipate that you will be sitting in the dark watching the film?

(Audience member: "Two hours?")

Right. So that translates to about one hundred and twenty script pages. So, you have got to tell your story in that amount of space. One element of style they will also look at when you send a script (if it is in the proper format) is how many pages it is at the end? They will often look at the end of your script before they begin reading to see how long is its. If it's 200 pages, they will not give it serious consideration.

So, now… let's talk about you. What do you do? You heighten what you have and start your story at the end. Just take the most compelling moment of you narrative, you can place it right up front and then show it to them… and when they want to know more, you give it to them, just a little bit at a time. It's okay to go slower then, like you are dropping breadcrumbs, because by then they will already be hooked. I think that sometimes we shouldn't study writing narratives and character to create movies. We should study how they make movie trailers.

You know what I'm referring to? A movie trailer is that one to three minute advertisement for an upcoming feature film? The idea behind them is of course is that they want you to see the trailer and compel you to come back and see the film. Sometimes it works and other times it doesn't. I want you to think about the ones that worked – the ones that mastered the art of the tease. Take a look at the trailers for:

Dark Knight (2008) https://www.youtube.com/watch?v=EXeTwQWrcwY

Jaws (1975) https://www.youtube.com/watch?v=U1fu_sA7XhE

Pearl Harbor (2001) that leads with a less than two-minute pitch on the Japanese attack on December 7, 1941. I remember seeing it in a movie theatre and thinking I definitely have to check that movie out. https://www.youtube.com/watch?v=Og6oaOJFenE

This is how we have to present our pitches and scripts – like they were trailers. If you are pitching, give them two of the most compelling minutes of story and character you have. At the end of it all, there can only be one answer. They will have to read the script to find out. If you are getting coverage on the script, give them most compelling front ten pages of story and character you have. Make your pitch or script your own trailer.

So, start your story at the end means taking that pivotal moment – the most important moment – the irrevocable moment of your story and begin with it. Think of the very successful motion picture *Titanic* (1998). It begins from the point of view of a survivor as the ship leaves South Hampton docks on a maiden voyage from which it will never return. This is an irrevocable moment, that sends the ship and all its passengers on a path from which many will never return. That's where you start your story. We don't need to see all of the narrative and character development that went before. Why? We get whatever we need of that as we go along. What about the survivor – how did she make it? You have to read the full script and find out. You hook them right there in the first ten pages or ten minutes of your film. That's your trailer. You also must create a sense of suspense. A reader might think, "this is the story of the ocean liner Titanic – I know what happened, it hit an iceberg and sank." And your screenplay might say, "maybe not this time, maybe not in this story" – you'll have to read further to find out. How many of you are familiar with the film *King Kong (1933, 2005)*? I don't know about you, but I always feel bad when a King Kong gets shot down and falls off the Empire State Building. I hope I'm not giving away the ending here for some of you?

  (Audience laughter – Catalano looks at one man in the front row)

You were going to go home and rent King Kong tonight… weren't you?

  (Audience member: "Yes… I wanted to find out what happens at the end.")

(Audience laughter)

I'm so sorry.

(Audience laughter)

But really, wouldn't it be nice to be surprised? Or at least taken to a place where you think that it just might be different this time. Just might. There is no rule that says these stories all have to end the way they end. So, when you start your reader at that pivotal moment, make them think that maybe this time, it's not going to go the way these stories always go? Maybe this one is different? I better read further because I need to know.

It's that same thing that happens when you're driving on the freeway – in Los Angeles it's the 405 Freeway and there is a traffic accident. You are sitting in backed up traffic even though the accident is on the other side of the freeway because all of the drivers in front of you have to slow down to take a look. Why? They all want to know. What do they want to know? Whatever it is… they want to see what happened as best as they can and get a sense of how it will all turn out. Once they pass the scene, there off on their way again full speed ahead. But they have to slow down to take a look. They all want to see that pivotal moment.

Your job as a writer is to give it to your reader in an interesting way. They don't need every single detail… just the essence. Now I'm going to as you all a question.

Ready?

20

Visualize your Book as a Movie Trailer

Start Your Story at the End

How many of you have ever asked a relative or a friend "How was your day?" Now if we look at that question for its face value you are asking them how their day was. But what you are really asking is for the high points or pivotal moments in their day. The important events that shaped the way they are "now" when you are speaking to them. They can answer you with a list of minute details beginning when they woke up brushed their teethe, went to the bathroom etc. or they can highlight the one or two things that happened that brought them to where they are at that moment. Which would you prefer?

(Audience – the highlights)

Exactly. Just a few of the bullet points of what you think is important and then I will make my own judgment of what I will want to explore further. The truth be know, not all facts are of equal importance at a given moment in time. So, your stories are in many ways the same thing. Just start them out with the most important aspects of your characters and story – then you can fill them in on what is needed as you go along. Writing is not like a court of law where you have to state all the facts of a particular story or person for a jury. Use just the elements of plot and character you need to create the desire of the reader or viewer to go further.

I'm thinking as I speak of the opening of the film *Jurassic Park* (1993). It opens with the cage of the Velociraptor being brought into frame. You hear the caged dinosaur within the cage as the camera pushes in closer and closer. That's all you need to know. This film is about dinosaurs – they're back and this one is a dinosaur you want to stay away from. But the book of the same title starts off quite differently. It opens with a couple and their child on the beach in Costa Rica – this was actually the opening for *Jurassic Park II (2001)*. The original film takes us right to where we need to be and pulls us in. We want to know what is in the cage and what will happen next?

Incidentally, I read an interview of Steven Spielberg about the making of the film Jurassic Park. As he tells the story, he was on the Universal lot and ran into Michael Critchton (the author of the Jurassic Park novel) who was working on the book. When he asked what he was working on, Crichton just said this: "Dinosaurs… they come back."

(Audience reaction)

That was it. Spielberg responded with something like "I'm in." Dinosaurs they come back or something like that and the rest as we say it is history. But the reason I mention this film's opening and pitch is because they are both examples of how to start your story at the end. You may argue that the opening cage scene was not really the ending. But I will say that it really was. Once the Velociraptor was introduced, it was a point of no return. All of the other plot points during the film about how the dinosaur DNA was captured to create new dinosaurs and the structure of the park are all expositional points that support the main idea… that dinosaurs come back. We watch the film or read the script and all of those vital points are provided along the way. But only those points which feed into the main premise of the story. This is a very different telling of event from when someone is asked how their day was and then rattles off every detail of every moment equally. We learn all the facts but really only the facts that matter within the framework of the story you have created.

So, by starting your story at the end, you become the editor of those plot points that you will share with your reader or audience. You can choose them specifically to support and then deliver your main premise. Starting at the end also helps to create dramatic tension. Why? You are bringing your audience in at a pivotal moment that connects with your audience with maximum impact. You hook your audience at the end and then make them a promise to show them how it wall all turn out if they take the journey with you.

That takes us back to creating a trailer. What is a trailer? It's a promise isn't it? It's a promise that says to an audience... if you come to see this movie, it will be a hilarious comedy, or a non-stop thriller, or a tragic love story. Those are promises. If I say to you "dinosaurs... they come back..." That is a promise. I am saying is that you will see dinosaurs... and not the kind you see in a museum that are all skeletons and still. These dinosaurs are alive... right now. It doesn't matter how they got here... that you will explain later. Right now, this is the promise. Are you on board?

Hopefully, the answer is yes. Once you put something down on paper, after you hone it down, edit it and make it perfect, you are giving what you created to another person. What happens then? You "hope" that they will like what you created. Hope is such a passive word... you "hope" that they will like it. I'd rather you create it from the point of view that you are making (through your writing) a promise to them that they can't refuse so that you can "expect" that they will like it. You have created a scenario that is inevitable. It is true that you can't control many of the elements that surround a submission, but you must expect that they will take your work on its face value and appreciate it. Now, it may not fit what they are looking for, but they will like what you create and you can live to fight another day.

Now whether they want to take your pitch or submission to the next step or not becomes only part of the process. If you are pitching, make your idea into one that is inevitable... dinosaurs they come back. Inevitable, because your listener will want to know how that can be... and if they want to know how, you've got them. If you are submitting your script, pull them in early on... within the first ten pages. Once you get them to page ten, they have reached the point of no return. They can't put the script down; they have to see it through to find out what happens in the end. Once you have them committed to your story and characters, you can find moments to slow down and give your project detail and texture. The hardest part in all of this is to get them on board and committed. That commitment takes place right up front. That is why I am saying start at the end. Start at your most pivotal moment.

If you are not sure how to accomplish this, put yourself in a darkened movie theatre watching a trailer of your book or screenplay. How would your create that, where would you start and what elements would you show an audience in two minutes or less that could pull them into your story?

Okay, let's stop for a moment here. I want all of you to take out a piece of paper. If you don't have one, there are blank papers right up here on the table. I want you to write down a two-minute trailer for your book or screenplay. Remember, I want you to think about your characters and story and in two minutes (about 300 words), break down at least seven bullet points of what an audience might see and here. Take your time... I will be grading these...

(Audience laughter)

Only kidding... You've got ten minutes... I'm such a slave driver aren't I?

(Ten minutes later)

Okay, do we all have something written down? If it's not complete, that's okay. We won't have time to read them all, but I wanted you to have the experience of taking your characters and story and trying to frame it in this manner.

(Audience member: "It's not easy.")

No it's not. This process sort of forces you to take a larger idea and compress it into a very small amount of time without losing the value of your creative idea. We should know a little something about your main characters then put them within a pivotal moment in your story. I just saw a hand go up? Yes.

(Audience member: Can I try mine?)

I thought you'd never ask.

(Audience laughter)

(Audience member stands up at his chair and reads.)

Trailer examples have not been included at the request of seminar participants. However, I am including a link for HOW TO MAKE

A BOOK TRAILER by Joanna Penn - http://www.thecreativepenn.com/2011/01/07/how-to-create-a-book-trailer/

Great job... on such short notice. This is an example of what we should all do for our projects. In a way, it forces you to think like a marketing person – you will have to answer questions like what kind of audience is my project best suited for? What is their age? Gender? Once you start to come up with those answers and you create a promise around what you have created, it is important to stay true to that premise.

Have any of you seen the new film called *The Reader (2008)*? Now the film itself is a good film, but I do have a little bit of a problem with the way it was presented in the trailers. It was marketed as a sort of Nazi film (a film about Nazi's) but it was actually something quite different. In the first three minutes of the film, the child becomes ill (I don't want to tell you the whole plot) – but what I will tell you is that the two major characters of the film are thrust together in a very compelling way that you want to find out what happens to them at the end.

What about *Slum Dog Millionaire (2008)* which starts at end – where you find the main character in police station in trouble and then you find out the rest of the story – the how, the what through the telling. You find out the important parts that answer the questions that you as a reader or audience member want to know. What am I saying then? I will be struck by lightening when I say this. You have to write like a "salesman!" You have to sell your idea to the audience or the reader. Create a situation where they will come on the journey with you because they want to... because they **have** to.

> (Audience member asks: "What about television? Isn't television written in a formula that would make it very difficult to start at the ending.")

Television is written in a rigid pattern of scenes and acts that must fit into a specific run time format. You have all heard the term "teaser" or "cold open."

> (Audience members respond, "Yes.")

That's how television starts at the end by going directly into the episode plot right at the opening of the show, before any opening credits. What do we see? A crime being committed, a murder, a UFO approaching earth from space, a young woman walking down a dark street at night and then the sound of someone following her – she turns back and sees no one, then starts to run but is grabbed from behind. We hear her screams echo out of the darkness as we cut to opening credits. The hope is, that we don't change the channel and we'll stay to find out what happened.

You know, as I say this, I'm also thinking of the CSI shows, that usually open with a crime scene where they go through some basic plot points detailing the crime... and then the coroner says something like... "Looks like a drive by...." And then a close up actor David Caruso with sunglasses saying, "Drive by Miami style..." Beat, and then the opening theme music and credits. http://www.televisiontunes.com/CSI_Miami.html

So in television, we can and do start at the end. However, what is different than film is that your characters and story unfold in smaller more specific blocks, which then take you to the resolution. Also, often in television, the characters are reoccurring, so their development is on going. We find out little bits and pieces about them over a much longer period of time if the format is episodic. Also while we are discussing other mediums besides novels and film, we should also mention the Internet.

The Internet offers lots of opportunity for writers to create content for a multitude of platforms. However, in most cases, the format is interstitial and the segments that are written are often shorter – maybe two to three minutes in length. If you have a story either in novel for or direct screenplay, you will have to work within a format that is similar to creating a mosaic. You will work with smaller pieces which separately must stand on their own (with respect to character and story) but also fit into a larger picture when assembled. I worked on a series, years ago for Fox Television called *The Adventures of Dynamo Duck* - http://www.imdb.com/title/tt0289050/

The story line as it appears in IMDB.COM is "The world's smallest and most feathered secret agent takes on the forces of evil and saves the world while wooing women and creating chaos around the globe." The show was actually a series of 2-3 minute episodes that Fox TV used as bumpers between programs. We had to create reoccurring characters out of little ducks and gerbils – but the stories would always be different. Each little episode, had it's own story line with a beginning and ending. But all of the episodes fit together like a mosaic to tell a larger story.

So think of your novels like food... (I love to talk about food)

(Audience laughter)

Your novel is Tuscany chicken.

(Audience laughter)

...and for an interstitial approach. You do it piece by piece. Here's a pea... here's a potato... just one... now a carrot

(Audience laughter)

You see, we are doing this piece by piece... and when we're done... we will have the whole dish. The whole Tuscany Chicken. All of it. So, you have to take your novel and break it into smaller segments that could be read as an audio file or read or performed by actors. The artistic way of describing it would as if it were a mosaic. But remember it's like eating Tuscany Chicken a piece at a time. Don't do this now... but when you are home... alone... take your novel, your idea, your screenplay and break it down into one hundred one minute segments or fifty-two minute segments and see how it would flow. The good news about the Internet is you can create that on your own. You don't really need someone to produce that for you. If you have a MAC (if you don't I'm so sorry)...

(Audience laughter)

If you have a MAC, you can, using Garage Band and a nice microphone, create interstitial episodes of your work and then put it up on the Internet. Why would you want to do that? First of all, it will be fun and secondly it will showcase your writing. When someone asks you what have you done, you can point them toward your Internet series.

21

Rosebud

Start Your Story at the End

So STARTING AND the end will help to create an interest in your work for the reader or the audience. We have also talked about writing for a particular medium whether it is cinema, television or the Internet. Also remember that all of these mediums are visual. Whereas theatre uses language to communicate its content and literature uses prose and metaphor, film and television are visual. So starting at the end in a screenplay may simply be showing a simple action. There is no requirement that there has to be a full-fledged scene with dialogue. In the classic film *War of the Worlds (1953)* – after credits the film opens with a large object crash landing near the small town of Linda Rosa. Once that object lands, strange things start to happen. So, we know all is not well and that something terrible is going to happen. But we don't know what. Sometimes all you have to do is show a particular pivotal moment without dialogue or character.

It could be a visual scene with a very small amount of dialogue. A man is led up the wooden stairs to a gallows and a noose is placed around his neck. The executioner asks: "Do you have an last words?" The man turns toward the camera and simply says: "You haven't heard the last of me." A black sack covers the man's head; a moment later the executioner pulls the lever and the condemned man is dropped through gallows doors. His body jerks uncontrollably and then he dangles there in stillness. The executioner pulls back the black sack revealing another man's face. Where did the condemned man go? Now a promise has been made here. What was it?

(Audience member: "That the dead guy was going to come back.")

Okay, how?

(Audience member: "Maybe as a ghost?")

We don't really know do we? All we know is that he is coming back and if we want to know how and when, we will have to read the script or watch the movie. Think of the movie *Citizen Kane (1941)* https://www.youtube.com/watch?v=-r0b_XeRkG4

The film opens at the end of the life of a person – as ominous music plays we see the following images:

A "No trespassing sign"

A fence

A larger ornate gate

As the camera pushes in we see the tattered grounds of what at one time was an enchanted place, monkeys in a cage, a water playground with gondolas and in the background at the top of a hill an enormous castle. As we push in closer we see only one window lit which then goes of, it is lit once again and we realize we are now inside the room as we push in further to see falling snow. Then it is revealed to be snow falling within a glass globe held in a hand.

Then a close up of Kane's lips and the word "Rosebud" he draws his last breath. The globe rolls out of the hand and down a step then crashes into many pieces. Through the broken piece of glass, we see the reflection of a nurse enter the room, then gently place and cover the body with a sheet.

Fade to black. This is what the audience experiences as they sit in a darkened theatre. Now what about the reader? How did the script written by Orson Welles and Herman J. Mankiewicz look?

PROLOGUE

FADE IN:

EXT. XANADU - FAINT DAWN - 1940 (MINIATURE)

Window, very small in the distance, illuminated.

All around this is an almost totally black screen. Now, as the camera moves slowly towards the window which is almost a postage stamp in the frame, other forms appear; barbed wire, cyclone fencing, and now, looming up against an early morning sky, enormous iron grille work. Camera travels up what is now shown to be a gateway of gigantic proportions and holds on the top of it - a huge initial "K" showing darker and darker against the dawn sky. Through this and beyond we see the fairy-tale mountaintop of Xanadu, the great castle a silhouette as its summit, the little window a distant accent in the darkness.

DISSOLVE:

A SERIES OF SET -UPS, EACH CLOSER TO THE GREAT WINDOW, ALL TELLING SOMETHING OF:

The literally incredible domain of CHARLES FOSTER KANE.

Its right flank resting for nearly forty miles on the Gulf Coast, it truly extends in all directions farther than the eye can see. Designed by nature to be almost completely bare and flat - it was, as will develop, practically all marshland when Kane acquired and changed its face - it is now pleasantly uneven, with its fair share of rolling hills and one very good-sized mountain, all man-made. Almost all the land is improved, either through cultivation for farming purposes of through careful landscaping, in the shape of parks and lakes. The castle dominates itself, an enormous pile, compounded of several genuine castles, of European origin, of varying architecture - dominates the scene, from the very peak of the mountain.

DISSOLVE:

GOLF LINKS (MINIATURE)

Past which we move. The greens are straggly and overgrown, the fairways wild with tropical weeds, the links unused and not seriously tended for a long time.

DISSOLVE OUT:

DISSOLVE IN:

WHAT WAS ONCE A GOOD-SIZED ZOO (MINIATURE)

Of the Hagenbeck type. All that now remains, with one exception, are the individual plots, surrounded by moats, on which the animals are kept, free and yet safe from each other and the landscape at large. (Signs on several of the plots indicate that here there were once tigers, lions, and giraffes.)

DISSOLVE:

THE MONKEY TERRACE (MINIATURE)

In the foreground, a great obscene ape is outlined against the dawn murk. He is scratching himself slowly, thoughtfully, looking out across the estates of Charles Foster Kane, to the distant light glowing in the castle on the hill.

DISSOLVE:

THE ALLIGATOR PIT (MINIATURE)

The idiot pile of sleepy dragons. Reflected in the muddy water -
the lighted window.

THE LAGOON (MINIATURE)

The boat landing sags. An old newspaper floats on the surface of the water - a copy of the New York Enquirer." As it moves across the frame, it discloses again the reflection of the window in the castle, closer than before.

THE GREAT SWIMMING POOL (MINIATURE)

It is empty. A newspaper blows across the cracked floor of the tank.

DISSOLVE:

THE COTTAGES (MINIATURE)

In the shadows, literally the shadows, of the castle. As we move by, we see that their doors and windows are boarded up and locked, with heavy bars as further protection and sealing.

DISSOLVE OUT:

DISSOLVE IN:

A DRAWBRIDGE (MINIATURE)

Over a wide moat, now stagnant and choked with weeds. We move across it and through a huge solid gateway into a formal garden, perhaps thirty yards wide and one hundred yards deep, which extends right up to the very wall of the castle. The landscaping surrounding it has been sloppy and casual for a long time, but this particular garden has been kept up in perfect shape. As the camera makes its way through it, towards the lighted window of the castle, there are revealed rare and exotic blooms of all kinds. The dominating note is one of almost exaggerated tropical lushness, hanging limp and despairing. Moss, moss, moss. Ankor Wat, the night the last King died.

DISSOLVE:

THE WINDOW (MINIATURE)

Camera moves in until the frame of the window fills the frame of the screen. Suddenly, the light within goes out. This stops the action of the camera and cuts the music which has been accompanying the sequence. In the glass panes of the window, we see reflected the ripe, dreary landscape of Mr. Kane's estate behind and the dawn sky.

DISSOLVE:

INT. KANE'S BEDROOM - FAINT DAWN -

A very long shot of Kane's enormous bed, silhouetted against
the enormous window.

DISSOLVE:

INT. KANE'S BEDROOM - FAINT DAWN - SNOW SCENE.

An incredible one. Big, impossible flakes of snow, a too picturesque farmhouse and a snowman. The jingling of sleigh bells in the musical score now makes an ironic reference to Indian Temple bells - the music freezes -

> *KANE'S OLD OLD VOICE*
> Rosebud...

The camera pulls back, showing the whole scene to be contained in one of those glass balls which are sold in novelty stores all over the world. A hand - Kane's hand, which has been holding the ball, relaxes. The ball falls out of his hand and bounds down two carpeted steps leading to the bed, the camera following. The ball falls off the last step onto the marble floor where it breaks, the fragments glittering in the first rays of the morning sun. This ray cuts an angular pattern across the floor, suddenly crossed with a thousand bars of light as the blinds are pulled across the window.

The foot of Kane's bed. The camera very close. Outlined against the shuttered window, we can see a form - the form of a nurse, as she pulls the sheet up over his head. The camera follows this action up the length of the bed and arrives at the face after the sheet has covered it.

FADE OUT:

This is a classic example of starting your story at the end. We can sit here today and know the significance of "Rosebud" the one word spoken at the opening of the story because we have the benefit of time. But let's try to imagine what audiences in 1941 thought when the film was first exhibited. The film is called Citizen Kane and is about the life of a fictional character Charles Foster Kane an extremely wealthy newspaper publisher. So where does the story start? At the moment that Charles Foster Kane draws his last breath and dies. His whispers only one word "Rosebud." If we want to find out why he says this word and about his life, we will have to invest our time in his story. Also, this is a perfect example of a "visual" way to start your story at the end. The audience and the reader are presented with a series of visual images which lead up to the one word spoken "Rosebud." Remember also, that your opening set up (starting at the end) does not have to be terribly long. I don't want you to feel as though you have to squeeze in an enormous amount of information up front. You are just trying to find the most pivotal moment and you will have plenty of time to fill in the blanks along the way with exposition.

22

WRITE LIKE A PAINTER

Start Your Story at the End

Here's another way of thinking about it. Imagine yourself as a painter and you have an idea for a painting. Have any of you ever painted before? I don't mean your house… a picture.

(Audience laughter)

Okay, so do we have any painters here today?

(Several hands go up)

Okay, so those who have painted did you have a visualization of how large or how small your final work would be?

(Audience member: "Yeah, I had to buy the canvass.)

So you had a general idea of how much literal space you would have to convey your idea. Whether it is large – the size of a whole wall or a small canvass – you had a pretty good idea of the amount of space you had to create your work. Now let's move over to writing. If you are writing fiction do those limitations apply? Do you have a sense of how many pages you will require to tell your story?

(Audience member: "For me, as long as it takes."

Okay, as long as it takes. Most of you agree?

(Audience agrees)

So you start to develop your story and you take as much time and page space as you need to bring it to its natural conclusion. However, when you transpose your story to another medium, you are suddenly confronted with specific formats and run time. You no longer can takes as long as it takes, you may have to make choices. Just like the painter who has to convey their work on the specific size of a given canvass. In this case, writing is just like painting.

We are taking that fictional work and converting into another medium. It could be any of the mediums we have discussed – film, television or the Internet. Now, assuming you are starting your story at the end – which may be totally different that what you have within your fictional work, you also have to consider run time and format requirements. I want you to think of your specific work.

Place your what is now the ending of your novel at the front of a screenplay. That's easy enough, now all you have to do is fill in the important plot and character elements along the way until you get to the end. But wait, you are about half way through the plot and character points from your book and you are already at 115 – 120 pages, you have run out of time and space. What do you do now? You think to yourself, I can reduce the font size to ten and that might buy me enough space to bring this story to a conclusion.

(Audience laughter)

Then you think again. Not even bringing the font down to ten will be enough. Maybe I can bring it down to eight-point font? That should do it. The real answer here is that you have to write for the medium and more importantly make choices. You have to figure out what are the most vital parts of your character and story to include in a screenplay. Also what parts of your character and story are the most visual so that they will work best in a film or television medium? If you are writing for cinema, your book has got to fit into an approximately two hour or 110-120 page time frame calculated at one page per minute of screen time. You may be thinking, that's not totally accurate. There have been films such as *Gandhi (1982)* at 191 minutes, *Dances with Wolves (1990)* at 236 minutes and *Titanic (1997)* at 210 minutes. There's no hard fast rule just a general practice and expectation about how long a film or screenplay should be. We can expand this expectation to audiences as well. Most people expect to be told the story in a movie generally within a two hour time period. Movie exhibitors such as Arclight, Regal, Cineplex or AMC also want to have films that are not too long so then can get as many showings in a given exhibition space (movie theatre) in a day. In today's market place when films or scripts go longer the run time is often cut down in their initial release and then the cut footage is put back after the theatrical release in DVD or streaming versions of the film. This works for a marketing standpoint as well because film companies can then take the cut footage and add it back in and sell us the same movie as what they call "the director's cut" or "the uncut version." Audiences wanting to see what was taken out, pay a second time for the same movie that had seen in the theatres. So this is a writing seminar about how to start your story at the end. What does all this have to do with my novel?

Everything. You have to take what you've labored on and make it shorter so that it is marketable. Through a process of selection, you must choose only those elements of your characters and story that are essential to your book and that work well visually for the film or television medium. You may be thinking, your asking me to turn my book inside out, start it at the end and then gut the story and characters to fit proper format for the medium? If I do that, I will lose the entirety of my book, my characters and story will be a shallow framework of the whole. It will not be as good. Does that ring a bell in your mind? People attending a film as the closing credits roll get up from their theatre seats and say "Good film, but I read the book and it was much much better!" The reason they say this is because they often are not getting all of the content that was in the original work. Choices had to be made to fit the work into the intended medium.

I am telling this to you because, if you choose to start your story at the end and you want to convert your book for film or television, you will have to make specific choices as to what you will include and what you will cut in your adaptation. That's the bad news if there is any. A lot of writers complain that they can't fit their book inside that framework. We talked about cinema, what about television, as we have said, the requirements there are a bit more rigid. If you want to convert your novel into a teleplay for a made for TV film with a two hour run time, that will convert to approximately eighty eight pages to take account for commercials and bumpers. For an hour-long show it is actually forty three to forty four pages.

(Catalano speaks to seminar administrator)
How am I doing on time so far? Okay, great.

(Audience member asks: "Is there any correlation between how many screen pages are contained in one of my novel pages.)

My guess, is there is going to be more than one screen page for each novel page for those pages of your book that you choose to adapt. But it really depends on how you choose to take what you have written in your book and place it within the screenplay.

In your book, you may have an elaborate description of a particular event, which takes, up most of your page. In the screen version, you may just take that same section and describe it in a sentence or two. Think about the opening of *Gone with the Wind (1939)* how the book opens:

Gone with the Wind, by Margaret Mitchell
Chapter 1

Scarlett O'Hara was not beautiful, but men seldom realized it when caught by her charm as the Tarleton twins were. In her face were too sharply blended the delicate features of her mother, a Coast aristocrat of French descent, and the heavy ones of her florid Irish father. But it was an arresting face, pointed of chin, square of jaw. Her eyes were pale green without a touch of hazel, starred with bristly black lashes and slightly tilted at the ends. Above them, her thick black brows slanted upward, cutting a startling oblique line in her magnolia-white skin — that skin so prized by Southern women and so carefully guarded with bonnets, veils and mittens against hot Georgia suns.

Seated with Stuart and Brent Tarleton in the cool shade of the porch of Tara, her father's plantation, that bright April afternoon of 1861, she made a pretty picture. Her new green flowered-muslin dress spread its twelve yards of billowing material over her hoops and exactly matched the flat-heeled green morocco slippers her father had recently brought her from Atlanta. The dress set off to perfection the seventeen-inch waist, the smallest in three counties, and the tightly fitting basque showed breasts well matured for her sixteen years. But for all the modesty of her spreading skirts, the demureness of hair netted smoothly into a chignon and the quietness of small white hands folded in her lap, her true self was poorly concealed. The green eyes in the carefully sweet face were turbulent, willful, lusty with life, distinctly at variance with her decorous demeanor. Her manners had been imposed upon her by her mother's gentle admonitions and the sterner discipline of her mammy; her eyes were her own.

On either side of her, the twins lounged easily in their chairs, squinting at the sunlight through tall mint-garnished glasses as they laughed and talked, their long legs, booted to the knee and thick with saddle muscles, crossed negligently. Nineteen years old, six feet two inches tall, long of bone and hard of muscle, with sunburned faces and deep auburn hair, their eyes merry and arrogant, their bodies clothed in identical blue coats and mustard-colored breeches, they were as much alike as two bolls of cotton.

Outside, the late afternoon sun slanted down in the yard, throwing into gleaming brightness the dogwood trees that were solid masses of white blossoms against the background of new green. The twins' horses were hitched in the driveway, big animals, red as their masters' hair; and around the horses' legs quarreled the pack of lean, nervous possum hounds that accompanied Stuart and Brent wherever they went. A little aloof, as became an aristocrat, lay a black-spotted carriage dog, muzzle on paws, patiently waiting for the boys to go home to supper.

Between the hounds and the horses and the twins there was a kinship deeper than that of their constant companionship. They were all healthy, thoughtless young animals, sleek, graceful, high-spirited, the boys as mettlesome as the horses they rode, mettlesome and dangerous but, withal, sweet-tempered to those who knew how to handle them.

Although born to the ease of plantation life, waited on hand and foot since infancy, the faces of the three on the porch were neither slack nor soft. They had the vigor and alertness of country people who have spent all their lives in the open and troubled their heads very little with dull things in books. Life in the north Georgia county of Clayton was still new and, according to the standards of Augusta, Savannah and Charleston, a little crude. The more sedate and older sections of the South looked down their noses at the up-country Georgians, but here in north Georgia, a lack of the niceties of classical education carried no shame, provided a man was smart in the things that mattered. And raising good cotton, riding well, shooting straight, dancing lightly, squiring the ladies with elegance and carrying one's liquor like a gentleman were the things that mattered.

In these accomplishments the twins excelled, and they were equally outstanding in their notorious inability to learn anything contained between the covers of books. Their family had more money, more horses, more slaves than any one else in the County, but the boys had less grammar than most of their poor Cracker neighbors.

It was for this precise reason that Stuart and Brent were idling on the porch of Tara this April afternoon. They had just been expelled from the University of Georgia, the fourth university that had thrown them out in two years; and their older brothers, Tom and Boyd, had come home with them, because they refused to remain at an institution where the twins were not welcome. Stuart and Brent considered their latest expulsion a fine joke, and Scarlett, who had not willingly opened a book since leaving the Fayetteville Female Academy the year before, thought it just as amusing as they did.

"I know you two don't care about being expelled, or Tom either," she said. "But what about Boyd? He's kind of set on getting an education, and you two have pulled him out of the University of Virginia and Alabama and South Carolina and now Georgia. He'll never get finished at this rate."

"Oh, he can read law in Judge Parmalee's office over in Fayetteville," answered Brent carelessly. "Besides, it don't matter much. We'd have had to come home before the term was out anyway."

"Why?"

"The war, goose! The war's going to start any day, and you don't suppose any of us would stay in college with a war going on, do you?"

"You know there isn't going to be any war," said Scarlett, bored. "It's all just talk. Why, Ashley Wilkes and his father told Pa just last week that our commissioners in Washington would come to — to — an — amicable agreement with Mr. Lincoln about the Confederacy. And anyway, the Yankees are too scared of us to fight. There won't be any war, and I'm tired of hearing about it."

"Not going to be any war!" cried the twins indignantly, as though they had been defrauded.

"Why, honey, of course there's going to be a war," said Stuart. "The Yankees may be scared of us, but after the way General Beauregard shelled them out of Fort Sumter day before yesterday, they'll have to fight or stand branded as cowards before the whole world. Why, the Confederacy —"

Scarlett made a mouth of bored impatience.

"If you say 'war' just once more, I'll go in the house and shut the door. I've never gotten so tired of any one word in my life as 'war,' unless it's 'secession.'

The screenplay version of it approaches the same material in shorter more concise way:

Gone With the Wind written by Barbara Keon, Ben Hecht, Oliver H.P. Garrett, John William Van Druten, Jo Swerling, Sidney Howard

Chapter 1 Scarlett's Jealousy

(Tara is the beautiful homeland of Scarlett, who is now talking with the twins, Brent and Stew, at the Doorstep.)

BRENT

What do we care if we were expelled from college, Scarlett. The war is going to start any day now so we would have left college anyhow.

STEW

Oh, isn't it exciting, Scarlett? You know those poor Yankees actually want a war?

BRENT

We'll show 'em.

SCARLETT

Fiddle-dee-dee. War, war, war. This war talk is spoiling all the fun at every party this spring. I get so bored I could scream. Besides, there isn't going to be any war.

BRENT

Not going to be any war?

STEW

Ah, buddy, of course there's going to be a war.

                    SCARLETT
    If either of you boys says "war" just once again, I'll go
    in the house and slam the door.

                    BRENT
    But Scarlett honey..

                    STEW
    Don't you want us to have a war?

                    BRENT
    Wait a minute, Scarlett...

                    STEW
    We'll talk about this...

                    BRENT
    No please, we'll do anything you say...

                    SCARLETT
    Well- but remember I warned you.

What you do with your particular book is really up to you. However, don't think of it as cutting from your novel, think instead of selection. You are selecting those portions of your work that will be fit the medium that you are intending to place your story and characters into. You will bring over as much as you need to. Remember that when we write, the creative process (like painting) is a solitary one. We sit in front of our laptops or yellow pads and we take what is in our imagination and put it down. This process is very much like painting. However, once it is completed, our work gets handed over to directors, actors, sometimes other writers and designers who take what we have created and add to it. This is probably why writers try to put as much as they can into a screenplay because they want the artistic input that follows to be as well informed as possible. We write in the detail because we want our vision to remain in intact. This is understandable but often a fruitless effort. The best we can do is write a compelling story with interesting characters and hope that most of what we put in is kept. But there is no guarantee and the more you write in will not make a difference. Film and Television are collaborative arts and there will always be the collective input of directors, writers and designers to you work. It is the nature of the creative process. And there is also the audience to consider.

23

Who is Your Target Audience?

Start Your Story at the End

Let me ask all of you this question. All of you sitting here today – if I were to say to you, the particular novel that you have in your back pocket – what is your target audience? Also I will not allow you to say "general." What audience is the best fit for your work?

(Audience member: "And you can't answer general?")

Right.

Let me help you a bit. You could say something like… adults eighteen to thirty… or adults eighteen to twenty three Let's talk about the age ranges that advertising agencies use when planning marketing campaigns:

12 – 17
18 – 24
25 – 34
35 – 44
45 – 54
55 – 64
65+

What about gender – do you feel your work is a better fit with women or men or does it matter? Now we're writers here today, not advertising agencies. But there is something that we can learn from this. I think it is important for you to know who the audience is for your work. Who is the most likely cross section of people that would be interested in what you are writing about? Some of you may be thinking, I just want to write a story and great characters – that will be enough for me. But I think you need to have an idea of who might be interested in your type of story. Why? Because it will be a question that will be asked somewhere down the line if it is considered for publication or production as a film or television. So now I'm asking you again. What audience is the best fit for your work?

> (Audience member: "I have a woman's story but it is best suited for a general audience.")

Okay, so it's a woman's story – that would probably have more appeal to women than men? Is that correct?
(Audience member: "Yes, I think so...")
I feel like an attorney cross-examining someone.
(Audience laughter)
Sir?

> (Audience member: "My work is kind of a middle class drama also general and can appeal to both men and women in the 25 to 45 age range.)

Okay, excellent. Now there is no science to this. But I think it's important that you know where your work fits into to the over all picture. This will make your job of selecting what will or won't work when you convert it over to a screenplay. It will also provide you with an answer if someone sitting across a desk at a pitch, or a reading asks you where it fits in. You can answer it with confidence. This understanding also will help you focus on "where" to take your screenplay once it is written. For example, if your work is a "woman's story" it might be a great fit for Lifetime Television or the WE channel. Why? Because Lifetime's base is women 18-49 – that's what their programming is most effective reaching. That might be a perfect place for your project to be developed. Then your thinking I want my project to be a major motion picture reaching millions of people. But know that a cable network like Lifetime reaches approximately 99 million viewers. Not bad...

I don't want you to leave this seminar thinking all I wanted to talk about was making your books into movie trailers and selling to specific markets. But as writers, in order for us to "play" in this world we are dependent upon others to buy and develop our works. So, selling or marketing whatever you want to call it is always going to be part of it unless you are planning to write your screenplay and just placing in on shelf in your living room. If you were a painter, you could paint your painting and then hang it up on the wall in your living room and then sit down with a glass of wine, look at it and enjoy it. But your script needs to be produced and that's where the selling comes in. We all write, and that's a given. But every once in a while, we get that phone call, letter or email when someone wants to read what we have created. That's why it's so important to know what we have and where it fits in. If that call comes from Lifetime, you kind of know then where you are going. If it's USA Network instead of Lifetime, you know that USC skews more toward male viewer and therefor their programming has more adventures, crime shows and action series. Once you know this, you don't rewrite your script, you just select and highlight different parts of it. It's what car salesmen do when you go into a showroom.

This is going to sound sexist but it is not intended to be that way.

(Audience laughter)

If a man enters the showroom and asks about tires, engine size and performance, the salesperson will focus on the mechanical and performance aspects of the vehicle. If a woman enters the showroom and sits in the seats, the salesperson will talk about safety, cup holders, comfort and economy. It's the same car, nothing has changed but which areas the salesperson highlights in his or her presentation. Now back to writing.

24

Start Your Story at the End

Start Your Story at the End

THIS IS WHAT you are going to do when you go home tomorrow.

1. Start your screenplay at the pivotal moment (at the end) that connects your reader to your characters and story.
2. Develop a plan to select those moments within your story to include in the screenplay. Those moments should be integral to your characters and story and collectively make your screenplay no longer than 110-120 pages long for film or 88 pages for a made for television movie.
3. Once you have completed your screenplay calculate who the audience is for this work. What is their age, gender and interests so you will know where to bring you screenplay when it is complete.
4. When marketing your screenplay, to specific outlets, describe only those portions of your story and character that fit with the given outlet. Develop a marketing plan for you work for each outlet.
5. Optional – create literally or in your mind a trailer or poster for your screenplay – what would be your promise to an audience?

The overall goal here is to create something that is visually clear and compelling for a reader or audience member. We want them to not put the script down because each moment or page leads them to the next until the ending. Also, when and wherever you can be visual – the more visual you are, the greater the chance you will have to pull them in. Do tell the story, but don't forget to paint the picture that shows them how it's going to be. And remember to do it as quickly as possible – or at least within the first ten pages.

(Audience member: "When you are setting up your book to be a screenplay, how much of the description do you keep?")

Not a lot. Only bring over what is essential to pull the reader in. Nothing more. You don't want to bog them down with description because your goal is to pull them into your story and characters. You don't want a lot of tedious description but you do want to describe your characters in setting in a such a way that you give them just enough and wanting more.

This is going to sound inappropriate but here goes. Now I want to say that I know absolutely nothing about stripping or pole dancing. I wrote a segment one time for, I think it was NYPD Blue and the producer said to me "you obviously have never gone to a strip club." And that is still true today. But here goes.

(Audience laughter)

If you are watching a stripper and they come up on the stage and take all their clothes off in ten seconds – then they are just dancing up their naked – this gets boring because there is no tension... no sense of mystery. But, if they get up there and dance and take one little piece of clothing at a time and just tease you – they create tension and interest. Why because we all want to see what they will reveal next. Am I right?

(Audience laughter)

Well writing in this case is like stripping. You give them what they need to pull them in, no more... no less. Your goal is to keep them interested and engaged. Once they make the commitment to stay then you have them where you want them. Your tools are description, dialogue and action and you want to use them a tautly as possible. No waste... every word you include counts toward your goal of keeping your reader engaged. Anything more should be cut. You don't want to cut the heart of your work – somewhere in the middle is the answer. I have an exercise you can try at home. Take ten lines of description from your book and boil it down to two without losing the tension, impact or meaning. Try that on a couple of passages to see how it feels.

Look I want to say that I love language and love using language in my writing. I am a playwright, and that is a medium where language is paramount. However, film and television are visual mediums and focus on what to "show" rather than "tell" and audience.

(Audience member: "Should we write in camera angles?")

No, do not. The director and director of photography will want to do their own visual rendition of your script. They will not follow your angles anyway. Just tell the story unless a specific camera angle is needed to convey the plot or character. I want to thank you all for being such a great group. I hope you enjoy the remainder of the Writer's Conference and I am available for any questions. Do I have any questions from anyone?

Stock tips? Recipes?

(Audience laughter)

(Audience member: "What about lighting?")

Only as it is needed to describe the ambience or setting of your work and if by mentioning it you heighten the dramatic moment. Do you remember our example of a woman walking down a dark alley who is strangled from behind? I think a bit more description of lighting would help that set up. However, with that said, you don't have to light every scene. I know as writers, we all want to do a good job setting the mood for the work and you could spend a page and half describing the light – how the sunrise cracked over the Tuscan hills. But in a screenplay, you have got to get to it. They will want to know that the setting includes the sun coming over the Tuscan hills but they don't want you to tell them how to create it.

> (Audience female member: "If you want it to be filmed in sepia – can you mention that?")

Yes, that's fine.

(Audience male member: "When you talk about the end in the beginning or working to it, you're not talking about giving away the end… are you?")

No, I'm talking about that pivotal moment just before. I don't want you to give away your ending. I want them to read your screenplay to find out how it will all turn out. I want you to take them right up to the edge of the cliff, I want them to feel their toes hanging off the edge, but they will have to read your screenplay to find out why your character is at the edge of a cliff and whether or not they jump. I want you to take them as close to the end as possible – start your story at that pivotal point.

(Audience member: "So you don't want them to know how it ends when you start?")

Exactly. Take them right up to it… make it compelling, very exciting, very now… very inevitable.

(Audience member: "What about stories in foreign countries – is there a market for that?")

Why not? As long as you have a clear idea of the demographic your work reaches and can connect that to an American market.

(Audience member: "One more quick questions about setting. Do you have to define where you are or can you define it as anywhere USA?")

The generality you speak of can be a good or bad thing. If anywhere USA supports your idea, then fine. If being a bit more specific helps your idea, I would add that detail.

Again, I want to thank you all. You have been a great group!
(Audience applause)
Thank you.

The First Ten Pages

SAN DIEGO STATE UNIVERSITY
25th Annual Writers Conference

HOW TO ADAPT YOUR NOVEL INTO A SCREENPLAY

BOOK 4

Frank Catalano

25

LOCATION LOCATION LOCATION

The First Ten Pages

I'M GOING TO say this. Screenwriting is a lot like real estate... "LOCATION – LOCATION – LOCATION. Location is everything. I live in Los Angeles and I went into the bank one day and while waiting on line I was talking to someone I knew about her screenplay. As we talked I noticed that there was a large amount to people listening to our conversation. Other people on line, the tellers and the management staff... in short everybody was interested in our conversation because it had to do with her selling her screenplay. When I saw this, I said in an elevated tone, how many of you people are in the process of writing or already a screenplay. After everyone laughed a bit a large group of those listening raised their hands. I thought to myself... my goodness... almost everyone has a screenplay!

(Audience laughter)

The reason why I'm telling you this story is to illustrate that almost EVERYONE in Los Angeles is either writing a screenplay, wants to write a screenplay or has a relative or roommate that has a screenplay.

(Audience laughter)

For those of you who do not live in Los Angeles this fervor for writing screenplays and the biz is more than likely not as intense.

Why am I asking where you live? Because I am trying to gage your availability to physically market your script in person. Bottom line is that everyone is either doing it or wants to do it and a lot of the communication between writer and producer is done face to face. So what about those of you who don't live in Los Angeles? How can you get your ideas heard and read?

(Audience member: "What about if you have an agent?")

When you say agent, do you mean literary agent for your fiction books?

(Audience member: "Yes.")

That's fine… but remember if your representation does not have a relationship with the person or producer they are trying to get to read your project, they too will be operating from a disadvantage. Also, location is a factor. If your agent is in North Carolina they will not have the same access that a local agency might have. So what you want to think about is how to get your idea or screenplay in front of someone who will give it the attention and consideration that it deserves.

So I thought that an interesting seminar might be about how to do that. Assuming you are not in the room with the reader because you are not in Los Angeles – what can you do to hook the reader and make them want to read the whole script? Now I keep referring to the "reader" as opposed to the term "producer." Why? In most cases, if you can get your script to be considered by a producer, that person will not be the person who actually reads your material. Submitted material is often "covered" by professional readers or production company staff assigned to that function. This person will read your script and then prepare a professional report about it. The term for this practice is called "coverage." When coverage is done on your script, it is essentially a report prepared by a reader that includes a 1-2 page synopsis of your story, character breakdown and an evaluation as to whether it merits further consideration. Sometimes the reader will also suggest above the line cast or director. The report, like Yelp, rates your work quantitatively by specific categories that may include: title, main characters, supporting characters, setting, plot, budget and commercial viability.

As a screenwriter you have several challenges.

1. Getting your script in front of someone to be read.
2. Getting the reader to like or be interested enough in giving your script their fullest attention rather than rejecting outright.
3. Getting positive coverage so that your script can move to the next level.

So how can you accomplish that? How can you get your script past the reader?

The answer is that you have to get them up front within the first ten pages. If you have them at that point, you will be more likely to keep them through the end of the work.

You more than likely won't have the opportunity to pitch your idea in person, so you have to do within the screenplay format. Have you ever had this happen to you? You get a response from a producer or agent that tells you that would like to see ten pages of your work?

They say something like: "Send over ten pages… and if we like it… we will call you."

(Audience members nod in agreement)

The hardest part for me has always been which ten pages to send? Do I select the rip-roaring climax of the story or a pivotal point in the plot or just send them the first ten? Now earlier this week, I did a seminar entitled START YOUR STORY AT THE END. I think a few of you were attended that seminar and the theory behind that statement START YOUR STORY AT THE END is based upon starting your work at the most pivotal moment in your screenplay. The most exciting moment that pulls in the reader or audience and has the greatest possibility that they will want to go further and read the entire work. So that answer to my question about which ten pages to send them is simple. Send them the first ten pages. But make those first ten pages create the desire for anyone reading them to want to go on to the end to find out what happens.

Now I'm saying this to all of you in this room. Those who live in Arizona… North Carolina… New York… Utah and even San Diego – if you don't have the opportunity to be there to be on your feet, in the moment pitching your story, then you have got to let your script do the work for you.

We live in an immediate gratification society… television and the Internet have done this to us. Our attention span is short. If we don't get what we are looking for right away, we do a mental check out. We may be going through the motions but we are not really connected. So we have got to make our connections soon and make them meaningful.

You don't have a lot of time to do this in. So I have set the arbitrary length of ten pages. That's your goal, to connect irrevocably in ten pages. Create an air of inevitability – after that, they will be connected and you will have them for the entire journey.

26

Creating Inevitability in the First Ten Pages

The First Ten Pages

One thing that we can all share in common is that we are all at one time or another members of an audience. We all are exposed to media... the movies, television and the Internet. Now I will ask you this. Put your audience hat on. Now, here's the question.

What about the first ten minutes or a motion picture or a television production? You sit there in a darkened room and experience the film or television show. Now think about how you reacted.

It's either you thought, this is interesting I want to experience more or this is boring and I'm thinking about eating a cookie. If it's television, you might reach over for the remote and just change the channel. One of my pet TV peeves is when the new crop of fall shows premiere. During the first few episodes of each show, the writers spend an inordinate time introducing characters and character relationships at the expense of plot. The net effect is that these early shows are relegated into tedious scenes of character development. This is probably why almost all of the new shows fail to gain an audience and are cancelled. I'd like the networks to spread out the seasons with longer runs of episodes so that each new show can develop their characters in an interesting way and by doing so build and audience.

Every season, there are usually one or two breakaway hits while the rest fade away. Ask yourself this, what about those hits attract us to them? What elements do we identify with? What elements do they have that makes us keep coming back and want to know more. If we can figure that out, we can include these elements in your screenplays. Please remember, if we didn't like the beginning we wouldn't be back again to make them a hit.

Same question for the movies… what elements are present in the first ten minutes of a feature film that pull us in? In my other seminars we talked about beginnings that pull you in and make you want to see more. For example, the opening of the motion picture *Jaws* (1975) with a classic opening that pulls you in. https://www.youtube.com/watch?v=yrEvK-tv5OI

It's nighttime on Amity Beach. Chrissy, a young girl runs along the beach toward the water followed by her inebriated male friend. As she gets closer to the water, she removes her clothing, he stumbles after her, and then falls head over heals into the sand. She jumps into the water and swims outward.

Then we see a close up of her head popping out of the water as she yells out "come in the water!"

The next time we see here is from the point of view of the shark – she swims peacefully in the water as the shark gets closer and closer – as it does the now famous music intensifies. Then we see Chrissy one last time smiling just before her legs get tugged and pulled below the water. Then she let's out a blood horrific scream as she is dragged across the water. Then there is one brief moment, where it looks like she might make it, she grabs onto a harbor buoy but is snapped away and disappears beneath the water. A moment later, all is quiet and serene on the beach and water. All this happens within the first three minutes of the movie. It pulls the audience in so that they have to see more to find out what it was that pulled Chrissy into the water and how it will all be resolved at the end.

Okay, that's the final film. Now, what did the screenplay JAWS by Peter Benchley and Carl Gottlieb – Based on novel by Peter Benchley look like for the same scene?

1   OVER BLACK   1

Sounds of the inner spaces rushing forward. Then a splinter of blue light in the center of the picture. It breaks wide, showing the top and bottom a silhouetted curtain of razor sharp teeth suggesting that we are inside of a tremendous gullet, looking out at the onrushing under- sea world at night. HEAR a symphony of underwater sounds: landslide, metabolic sounds, the rare and secret noises that certain undersea species share with each other.

CUT TO

2   <u>EXT. LIGHTHOUSE - NIGHT</u>   2

Caught in its blinding flash, the light moves on, fingering the fog. A lone buoy dongs somewhere out at sea.

3   <u>EXT. AMITY MAINSTREET - NIGHT</u>   3

The quaint little resort town is quiet in the middle of the night. A ground fog rounds a corner and begins spreading toward us. It fills over sidewalks and streets like some Biblical plague.

4   EXT. THE SOUTH SHORE OF LONG
    ISLAND - NIGHT   4

It is a pleasant, moonlit, windless night in mid-June. We see a long straight stretch of white beach. Behind the low dunes are the dark shapes of large expensive houses. The fog that has reached Amity proper is seen only as a low-hanging cloud that is pushing in from the sea. HEAR a number of voices sing- ing. It sounds like an Eastern University's Alma Mater.

5   ANOTHER ANGLE – BEACH   5

A bonfire is blazing. Gathered around it are about a dozen young men and women who are merrily trading fight songs from their respective universities. Two young people break away from the circle, Chrissie almost pulling a drunk and disorderly Tom Cassidy behind her.

6   CLOSEUP - CASSIDY   6

makes a clumsy try at kissing Christina but she laughs and ducks away.

7   ANOTHER PART OF THE BEACH   7

The fire, now one hundred yards in the b.g., silhouettes Chrissie running up a steep dune.

Once there, she pauses to look at the ocean that we can only hear. Cassidy plods up the dune behind her, grossly out of shape.

Chrissie runs down a few steps, leaving Tom Cassidy reeling on the summit. Chrissie's dress, bra and panties fly toward Tom, who can't make a fist to catch them. The dress drapes over one half of his head. Soggily aroused, Cassidy struggles to get his shoe off.

But Chrissie is already in full flight toward the shore. In she goes, a delicate splash, surfacing in a cold ocean that is unusually placid. Chrissie pulls with her arms, drawing herself into deeper water.

That's when we see it. A gentle bulge in the water, a ripple that passes her a dozen feet away. A wave of pressure lifts her up and eases her down again. Her face shows the beginning of fear. Maybe it's Tom. She smiles and looks around for him, then her eyes go to the beach where Tom – too drunk to stand – one pant leg off, is struggling with his other shoe. Chrissie turns and starts for shore.

8	CLOSE - CHRISSIE	8

Her expression freezes. The water-lump is racing for her. It bolts her upright, out of the water to her hips, then slams her hard, whipping her in an upward arc of eight feet before she is jerked down to her open mouth. Another jolt to her floating hair. One hand claws the air, fingers trying to breathe, then

> *it, too, is sucked below in a final and terrible jerking motion.* HOLD *on the churning froth of a baby whirl-pool until we are sure it is over.*

9   ANGLE - CASSIDY   9

> *in his undershorts, laughing, turning in slow stoned circles, a prisoner in his orange windbreaker that seems to have him in a full Nelson. He stumbles to his knees.*

As we read this today, we do so with the knowledge of the story and characters. However remember, when this story was first presented the reader and the audience did not have the familiar knowledge of JAWS and were spellbound by its story and characters. Stephen Spielberg took the basic idea that was included in the screenplay and the elaborated upon it – gave it tension and a sense of irony. However, the bottom line, is this opening compels us (even today) to want to know more, want to see more and ultimately find out what happens in the end. Think about the opening first ten pages of your script as if it were a movie trailer – a compacted version of what is to come.

If you are wondering how to do this?

Think about starting your script as if it were a movie trailer.

27

Let's Go to the Movies

The First Ten Pages

Okay, so why would I want to frontload my screenplay with all the important elements of my story in the first ten pages?

If I do that, what will there be left to tell?

And why would I want to make my wonderful screenplay into a movie trailer?

Good questions and the answer for them all is the same.

So that you hook the person reading your script and you make them want (have to) read the rest of through to the end.

Let me ask you this… what is the purpose of a movie trailer?

(Audience member: "To get you to go see the movie.")

Right and if you think about it. They are asking you to see the movie not immediately but sometime in the near future. How do they do that?

They make you a promise through the two to three minutes they have your attention.

If you see this movie it will be

A nail-biting thriller

A horror film that will frighten you

A love story that will make you cry

And they go one step further

They take what is unknown (you haven't seen it) and connect it to what is known that you are familiar with. We are familiar with stars, directors or Sequels (a continuation of a storyline and characters we already know).

A love story starring Brad Pitt – you may not know the story but you know Brad Pitt

A movie from Woody Allen – you may not know the story but you are familiar with Woody Allen's work.

The Expendables 1, 2 or 3 – does it really matter what the story is? You are familiar with all of the stars in the film and you know it will be an action picture.

So a movie trailer is a market tool used to connect an audience to a particular film at some future time.

Trailers pull us in with specific sounds and music to set the mood. Hard cutting so that they show us bits and pieces here and there but never truly reveal the entire plot. In short trailers tease us… into wanting more. Wanting more…

Everybody wants more of what they like. This makes me think of one of the greatest showman that ever lived Florenz Ziegfeld – who is best known for his Ziegfeld Follies. Now remember, Ziegfeld produced at the turn of the century in America – this was a time when there was a great formality in the way people behaved and dressed. But Ziegfeld was a master at knowing what the people wanted. So he came up with an idea to feature a half naked muscle man named Eugen Sandow to pose in a G-string on the stage. He was as naked as you could get without getting arrested. Of course women of the day, flocked to see THE GREAT SANDOW and some of them were even allowed to come up on the stage and squeeze his muscles – after which they promptly fainted. Ziegfeld knew how to pull an audience in and make them stay. He knew that no mater what he did, sex would sell to audiences at that time. So that's what he did.

Now back to our screenplays. In our first ten pages we want to do pretty much the same thing. Introduce some compelling aspects of your character and story – but never give it all away. Remember the GREAT SANDOW – just give them enough to hook them and want more. Once you have them there – they will stay until the end. Also, think about JAWS – we never see the shark. We knows something is down beneath the water but we really don't know what. If we want to find out, we have to stay with the story and characters.

You I can't help but think of the opening sequence of the feature film *The Godfather (1972)* which opens with the haunting melody of the Nino Rota Theme and then is followed with the close up on Bonesera the undertaker asking for the Godfather's help and more specifically "justice." https://www.youtube.com/watch?v=OIBpHO1gZgQ

Here is the opening scene written by Mario Puzo and Francis Ford Coppola in script form.

INT DAY: DON'S OFFICE (SUMMER 1945)

The PARAMOUNT Logo is presented austerely over a black background. There is a moment's hesitation, and then the simple words in white lettering:

THE GODFATHER

While this remains, we hear: "I believe in America." Suddenly we are watching in CLOSE VIEW, AMERIGO BONASERA, a man of sixty, dressed in a black suit, on the verge of great emotion.

BONASERA
America has made my fortune.

As he speaks, THE VIEW imperceptibly begins to loosen.

BONASERA
I raised my daughter in the American fashion; I gave her freedom, but taught her never to dishonor her family. She found a boy friend, not an Italian. She went to the movies with him, stayed out late. Two months ago he took her for a drive, with another boy friend. They made her drink whiskey and then they tried to take advantage of her. She resisted; she kept her honor. So they beat her like an animal. When I went to the hospital her nose was broken, her jaw was shattered and held together by wire, and she could not even weep because of the pain.

He can barely speak; he is weeping now.

               BONASERA
*I went to the Police like a good American.
These two boys were arrested and brought
to trial. The judge sentenced them to three
years in prison, and suspended the sentence.
Suspended sentence! They went free that very
day. I stood in the courtroom like a fool, and
those bastards, they smiled at me. Then I
said to my wife, for Justice, we must go to The
Godfather.*

By now, THE VIEW is full, and we see Don Corleone's office in his home.

The blinds are closed, and so the room is dark, and with patterned shadows. We are watching BONASERA over the shoulder of DON CORLEONE. TOM HAGEN sits near a small table, examining some paperwork, and SONNY CORLEONE stands impatiently by the window nearest his father, sipping from a glass of wine. We can HEAR music, and the laughter and voices of many people outside.

               DON CORLEONE
*Bonasera, we know each other for years, but
this is the first time you come to me for help. I
don't remember the last time you invited me to
your house for coffee...even though our wives
are friends.*

               BONASERA
*What do you want of me? I'll give you any-
thing you want, but do what I ask!*

               DON CORLEONE
And what is that Bonasera?

BONASERA whispers into the DON's ear.

DON CORLEONE
No. You ask for too much.

BONASERA
I ask for Justice.

DON CORLEONE
The Court gave you justice.

BONASERA
An eye for an eye!

DON CORLEONE
But your daughter is still alive.

BONASERA
Then make them suffer as she suffers. How much shall I pay you.

Both HAGEN and SONNY react.

DON CORLEONE
You never think to protect yourself with real friends. You think it's enough to be an American. All right, the Police protect you, there are Courts of Law, so you don't need a friend like me. But now you come to me and say Don Corleone, you must give me justice. And you don't ask in respect or friendship. And you don't think to call me Godfather; instead you come to my house on the day my daughter is to be married and you ask me to do murder...for money.

BONASERA
America has been good to me...

DON CORLEONE
Then take the justice from the judge, the bitter with the sweet, Bonasera. But if you come to me with your friendship, your loyalty, then your enemies become my enemies, and then, believe me, they would fear you...

Slowly, Bonasera bows his head and murmurs.

BONASERA
Be my friend.

DON CORLEONE
Good. From me you'll get Justice.

BONASERA
Godfather.

> DON CORLEONE
> *Some day, and that day may never come, I would like to call upon you to do me a service in return.*

Here in this one scene we are provided with a glimpse of what is to come. The scene is compelling because we are only seeing bits and pieces and want to know more – we have to know what is going to happen next.

28

INSTANT GRATIFICATION

The First Ten Pages

TELEVISION HAS CHANGED us irrevocably and we have come to expect everything we experience to happen immediately. We are not interested as much any more in the process but are more focused upon the result. We have connected instant gratification to pleasure.

Just give it to me now. I don't want to wait. We we are not fulfilled we become stressed out, unhappy and tense. To make matters worse, we fuel our instant gratification with the help of the latest technological device. Our IPhone, Blackberry, Ipad and Cloud give us everything we need at a moment's notice. If it takes to long, we pass on it. Think of the prologue for the Shakespeare tragedy ROMEO AND JULIET. The prologue like a movie trailer, kind of sets the audience up for what is about to happen on the stage.

PROLOGUE

Two households, both alike in dignity,
In fair Verona, where we lay our scene,
From ancient grudge break to new mutiny,

Where civil blood makes civil hands unclean.
From forth the fatal loins of these two foes
A pair of star-cross'd lovers take their life;
Whose misadventured piteous overthrows
Do with their death bury their parents' strife.
The fearful passage of their death-mark'd love,
And the continuance of their parents' rage,
Which, but their children's end, nought could remove,
Is now the two hours' traffic of our stage;
The which if you with patient ears attend,
What here shall miss, our toil shall strive to mend.

Now take that prologue today and try to put it in front of a feature film and audiences will say the following:

1. Get to it!
2. Can you show it to me instead?
3. Is the rest of this play going to be like this with long speeches?

Audiences will say "Okay, great… I'm outta here!"

(Audience laughter)

They would leave the theatre because the would say, that the prologue pretty much tells them what is going to happen and now that they know that why should they stay to see it.

You see what I am saying is that the audience doesn't care much about the process and the use of language – they are more concerned with the result and the ending. So you have to provide them with a pivotal moment but you don't show them how it turns out.

That's what we see in JAWS or THE GODFATHER.

So what I want to explore with you this morning is how you can take your novel or screenplay and find that pivotal moment of no return within the first ten pages of your script. A pivotal moment that will make your reader not want to put the script down. If that is the case, it won't matter if you have a pitch session or not. They will want to read your work until the ending. They will have no choice but to do so.

We want to create that hook in the first ten pages so they can't put it down. Not everyone will care or want to know about your story.

Yesterday, we talked about a writer who pitched a story idea (his only story idea) about the Russians landing on the moon first.

> Producer: What have you got?
>
> Writer: The Russians
>
> Producer: What about the Russians?
>
> Writer: They landed on the moon first.
>
> Producer: Okay.
>
> Writer: …and nobody knows about it!
>
> (Brief silence)
>
> Producer: Who cares … what else have you got?
>
> (Audience laughter)

That was it. The pitch was over and the writer left the room broken hearted. But what we can learn from this is that not everyone is going to love what you write. But if you write a compelling first ten pages with interesting characters and plot – you stand a chance to find someone.

What key elements of character and story must you have then in these first ten pages?

You have to provide them with character as in the example of the GODFATHER.

How many of you have gone to a film and we are all an audience. In the first ten minutes you don't have a clue as what is going on in the movie? Think about how you felt during those ten minutes – and you may have thought about leaving the movie. But then you think that you have paid for it so you stick it out. Now a reader, doesn't have that problem. If your script bores them, they just read it a lot faster or they skim and then write their report.

Sometimes even the trailers do not connect to our interests. We sit in the movie theatre and say to ourselves. "That one looks good." Then the next one comes one and we think "No way, Jose!"

(Audience laughter)

Or... I'll wait for HBO. That means I won't even stream it on pay per view for $5.99... I'll wait for it to come out on something I already pay for.

(Audience laughter)

(Audience member raises their hand)

Yes?

(Audience member: "What do you think of the film opening for *Inglorious Bastards (2009)*? What do you think about the first ten minutes?"

http://vimeo.com/67348832

Yes, I think this particular opening is exactly what I am talking about. This opening on its face value is a very simple meeting between a Nazi officer and a farmer but under its surface is filled with tension and terror. It doesn't hit you right over the head but the tension builds continually until the SS officer kills them all. Well, all except one.

With out that tension and immediacy we are doomed to disconnect. Our mind will take us somewhere else as it wanders away. We think of food (that's what I do), what we will do later that day, things we have to do the next day – all of it. From time to time we might reconnect to the characters and story but as time goes on even that becomes harder to do. We are all part of the instant gratification crowd. Just think about the last time your Internet connection was slow. As that small line moved across the computer screen indicating how much time was left, you felt like your brain was going to explode.

"I can't believe this! It's taking two minutes to download this file! Two minutes!" We become obsessed with the speed of it all and forget that we may be connecting to another machine on the other side of the world!

(Audience laughter)

…and although only a few of you sitting here today will admit that you go into one movie at a multiplex – get board, leave and go into another movie in the same theatre.

(Audience laughter)

We all do it. We as writers have to get to it sooner and make it more compelling than ever before. We do it for our audience and readers but we also do it for ourselves. This conference here today is not one for Dentists – we are not talking about teeth or dental hygiene… we are talking about writing. But here's the rub.

You don't need a degree like a dentist to call yourself a writer. Whether or not they are really a writer is not the point. The point is that they all call themselves a writer. Hollywood, is filled with bank tellers, former hairdressers and maybe even a few dentists that call themselves writers. They all have a screenplay or a book and a story that they want to tell. If they don't have that, they have an idea… and Hollywood is filled with people that want to tell their story. In all fairness to the producers and readers, there are a lot of people trying to peddle screenplays in Hollywood. So if they act a little standoffish, please understand that's why they feel this way. Think of this about 30,000 – 50,000 scripts are registered with the Writer's Guild of America (WGA) each year. Then there are new writers who don't bother to register their work with the WGA that brings the numbers closer to 100,000. Out of that number only a handful – maybe fifty are ever moved into development. Now wait, I don't want you all to get up and leave thinking if all that I am saying is true, then why bother.

However, with all of those numbers, I am telling you that you can enhance your chances to be one of those few screenplays that are put into development by making your work more inevitable. What does inevitable mean? Oxford dictionary defines it as "Certain to happen."

You can make your script inevitable by creating interest, connection and loyalty to your idea. I am talking about loyalty beyond reason. Have you ever heard someone say… "I just love that movie… I loved it so much I want to see it again!" When someone loves something that is loyalty beyond reason. How do they get to love? They have a connection to the idea that goes beyond the ordinary, which connects, to them in an intellectual, emotional, physical or spiritual way.

You're thinking to yourself right now: "I could do that… I could really do that. But how can I? I can't even get anyone to even look at my work. So, how could they ever be connected?"

How many of you have an agent that represents your writing?

(Several audience members raise their hands)

Out of those of you that have literary agents, how many have had a script sold through the auspices of this agent.

(No hands)

None? Okay, I'm not surprised because it is very difficult for an out of town representative to get material read because they are in the publishing side of the business not the entertainment side of the business.

Yesterday, in the workshop seminar we did there was a very nice woman who told me that an agent represented her and that she liked her agent very much. However, although she liked the person who was her agent, she was totally disappointed in them. They weren't get her books read or sold. So, for those of you who are sitting here today in despair because of what I am telling you, don't feel bad if you don't have an agent.

I'd rather have "no" agent than one who is not or cannot get me results. Why don't they get results? Maybe they are only effective in certain areas of specialization or maybe they only have contacts at some publishers or maybe they are not very good at what they do. In any case that's not a problem for you because you are going to develop and idea – a book – a screenplay that is inevitable.

The only thing you need to do is to get your work out there by any means that you can. The universe will take care of the rest. Don't worry about rejection. Every time you get a "no" it brings you closer to "yes."

29

WRITE LIKE YOU'RE A POLE DANCER IN A STRIP CLUB

The First Ten Pages

WE ARE ALL an audience. We said that. But we are all also consumers. Every morning when we get out of bed until we set our heads down at night – we are barraged with a cacophony of images and messages. These messages ask us: to buy certain items, to do certain things or behave in a certain way. A lot of you sitting here today are saying to yourself "Not me... I am not swayed at all." However, what if I say to this to you?

"Winston tastes good..." You would say?

(Audience: "Like a cigarette should!")

You know how old that slogan is? Probably the 1950's and they stopped running it in the early 1970's. But yet we still know it today. Even if we don't smoke. Why? Because it was hammered into our consciousness remorselessly in print, radio and television ads. So we know the slogan by heart and could even say that there is certain inevitability in it. That's what we have to do with our writing. We have got to get it out there no matter what and make it inevitable that it will be produced. They will have no other choice.

(Audience laughter)

Doesn't this sort of sound like one of those motivational seminars. In a way it is, I want you to commit to creating an exciting, compelling and inevitable first ten pages to your work. Why? Because you can do it and because you **should** do it! So let's stop thinking of ourselves as just writers. Let's also think of ourselves as consumers. When we are exposed to those remorseless ads that somehow take root in our minds – what are we actually exposed to?

A promise. No matter what we hear or see or taste or smell or touch, a promise is made to us. Buy this and your teeth will be whiter, do this and you will be thinner or smarter or look younger. Isn't that true?

(Audience nods in agreement)

So what if we were to write that way in the first ten pages of our work? Let your title and the first ten pages of your work intrigue the reader with a promise and take them right up to the moment when you will deliver that promise – but then don't fulfill it. Now I'm going to be inappropriate – just for a moment. Write your first ten pages as if you were a pole dancer in a strip club.

(Audience laughter)
I bet none of you thought I would ever say anything like that.
(Audience laughter)
Now I want to say that I know absolutely nothing about stripping or pole dancing. Is anyone here today a pole dancer or stripper?
(Audience laughter)
Just checking... could be your day job... or night job.
(Audience laughter)

I wrote a segment one time for a very popular television series that I will not name. I was asked to write a short scene in a strip club. So I did and when it was finished we read it and the producer said to me "you obviously have never gone to a strip club." And that is still true today. But here goes... I'm going to use this as an example.

(Audience laughter)

If you were watching a stripper and they came up on the stage and took all their clothes off in ten seconds – then would be just dancing up their naked – it would get boring because there would be no tension or no sense of mystery. Just a naked body on a pole going up and down... am I right?

(Audience laughter)

But, if they got up there and danced and took one little piece of clothing off at a time and just teased you – to see what you could through the see through mesh... they would create tension and interest. Why because we all want to see what they would reveal next.

(Audience laughter)

Well writing in this case is like stripping. You give them what they need a little at a time to pull them in, no more... no less. You need to write like you're a pole dancer in a strip club.

(Audience laughter)

No, really. Your goal is to keep them interested and engaged. You take them all the way through to page ten and the BANG! You stop. They are caught off guard and don't know what to do. All they know is the want... they have to see the rest. GIVE IT TO ME! You will "give it to them" but they will have to read the rest of your manuscript to get there.

Once they make the commitment to stay then you have them where you want them. Your tools are description, dialogue and action and you want to use them a tautly as possible. No waste... every word you include counts toward your goal of keeping your reader engaged. Anything more should be cut. You don't want to cut the heart of your work – somewhere in the middle is the answer. I have an exercise you can try at home. Take ten lines of description from your book and boil it down to just two lines without losing the tension, impact or meaning. Try that on a couple of passages to see how it feels.

(Audience member: "Aren't you cutting everything out of it?" No...

(Audience member: "For the sake of brevity?")

No you shouldn't lose any of the original impact of your writing. In fact it becomes, if anything, more compelling. These opening ten pages are where you draw them into your characters and story.

- Let the reader know your location and setting
- Introduce your main characters
- Set up your premise. Give them an inkling of what is to be... just a peek (like the stripper.
- Set the tone of the piece – just like you would with a piece of music and give them a hint of how it might end.

A good example is *Saving Private Ryan* (1998). The film opens with a cemetery scene and the hard cuts immediately into the American landing on Omaha Beach. You really get the end of the story and major character in the first three minutes of the film. As he makes his way, with his family following, to a specific grave, he finds it and tears well in in his. A moment later, literally through his eyes, we are transported back in time to D Day and Omaha Beach. In about the fourth minute of the film, we are introduced to the main character of the film Captain Miller (Tom Hanks). The rest of the movie takes the audience on a journey to that one moment at the cemetery.

https://www.youtube.com/watch?v=0HUf68gFGEE

So we have two elements operating here.

1. We create a compelling beginning in the first ten pages of the script. We introduce our main characters and story and create a sense of inevitability wanting our reader and audience to want to see it through to the end
2. We create a promise. What is a promise? It is an agreement to provide something in the future. If we set up our story as a thriller, a war movie, a romance. We have then to deliver that promise through to our ending. If we fail to do that, we have a problem.

I bought a book many years ago called THE NEXT TEN THOUSAND YEARS. I bought it on a rainy day like this, thinking that I would curl up and get a glimpse of the future. Where ever I was at the time (think I was in a hotel and there wasn't a great selection of books, so I figured what the heck? I'd like to know about the next ten thousand years.

(Audience laughter)

So, now I'm reading the book and am about half way through it, I realized that the book and its writer were a little bit crazy. As I read each chapter of the book, the premise of the next ten thousand years seemed farther and farther away. When he got to the chapter when they were going to dismantle Jupiter, I had enough and threw the book across the room against the wall where it remained until I checked out.

(Audience laughter)

Why was I angry? I will tell you. Because the promise on the cover of the book and the title stated that it was going to show me what it would be like in the next ten thousand years. Once I got half way through the book I realized that the promise made to me was not going to be kept. So I felt ripped off. I bought this book and the promise was not kept. The title and illustrated cover of space ships in space promised to tell how it was going to be in the future and then did not. Also, my time was wasted.

What does this story have to do with us? When we write our novel and then our screenplay there is an implicit promise made to an audience or reader. It starts with our title and then it begins with our very first page. When you think of your book or screenplay I want you to think about what your promise is to your audience. I would rather you have this clearly in your mind than a log line. I hate when they ask you: "What's your log line?" I hate the idea of an artificially cute log line that is designed to give the reader an idea (in a line) of what your story is about. I'd rather you tell them your promise. If you read this, this is what I promise you. I like this better. We can do log lines all day and they mean nothing.

    Producer: What's your log line?
    Writer: Moby Dick…

Producer: Right.
Writer: In outer space.
Producer: Great!
(Audience laughter)

What does that mean? I'm not sure. Our stories and characters are not served by a log line. Give the producer or reader something they can understand rather than reducing your work to a label or slogan. Instead, read my screenplay or invest in me and I promise you this will be an adventure you will never forget for the rest of your life. Or invest in me as a writer. If you don't like this script I have ten more stories I can talk to you about. Become that person, the one who writes the nail biting thrillers, the adventures or romantic love stories. Think of the late Nora Ephron was best known for her romantic comedies and was nominated three times for the Academy Award for Best Writing for *When Harry Met Sally (1989)*, *Sleepless in Seattle (1993)* and *Julia Julia (2009)*. You can develop a promise around yourself for certain types of stories and characters.

Make a promise to your audience and keep it. Which takes us back to our pole dancer in a strip club. What does a pole dancer promise us? This goes back to our first premise. They promise us that we will see and experience something in the future. They take us through the motions bit by bit until the end. Let's change the way things are done.

30

THE ROAD NOT TAKEN

The First Ten Pages

As I said, at the start of our seminar today, I have had the opportunity to spend time at many of the large motion picture studios in Hollywood. I spent the longest time at Warner Brothers and had a reverence for all of the great films that had been created there during the golden age of Hollywood. As a small Italian child living in New York, I had an uncle that was a film collector and he taught me everything about Hollywood and movies. My uncle Marty loved movies so much that he built a small theatre in his home. I am talking about a real movie theatre with a screen, velvet seats and a stage. As a young child he would let me sit in the theatre by myself and play great films with great stars. I would see the likes of Errol Flynn, Humphrey Bogart, Betty Davis and Gary Cooper over and over again. These films and the studios they were created in became something that I loved and respected. So when I arrived at the Warner lot, I was very excited about the tradition that studio had. I knew most of the films they had ever made and I believed that it was a magical place.

What I didn't know was that Warners and other majors like 20th Century Fox, Paramount, MGM and Universal were modeled after major manufacturing companies such as GM and Ford. The old-line studio chiefs ran the production in the studios in Hollywood and the New York offices ran the business of movie distribution and exhibition. I always looked at the movie business as an art but really it was also a business and Warner Brothers was no difference. Back in the golden age of Hollywood, the major studios released 52 films per year for audiences all around the world. This is something we as writers can never forget. That the way things are done at major studios is driven by business over art. It doesn't mean that studios will make anything for a buck. They want to make quality product but the drive for the bottom line will always win over the drive for the creative hallmark. The old system was what they called a contract system where everyone was hired and put on contract. Today, it is a freelance system, where writers, producers and actors (above the line) are brought in for a particular project or series of projects and often are profit participants in that endeavor.

So movie producers and by extension producers want quality product that an audience will want to spend money on and see. I think we need to rethink the way we approach them. Let's start a new way of doing things. Let's develop our projects less on the creative level and more on the business level. If your novel has sales, which are respectable, that means there are people willing to spend money to read your story and characters. Perhaps one way to describe our work then is from a marketing approach – detailing the target audience segment and profit viability. I know you probably all hate what I'm saying but let's start a new of doing things. Let's think like we are producers – so that we can answer those questions in a producer's mind that will come up when there is coverage done on your novel or script.

Some ideas tug and the heart while other have an intellectual appeal. Have both areas covered. When you get back home after this weekend. Look at your work again from a fresh point of view. Pretend you are a producer and evaluate your own work on its strengths and weaknesses for reaching a certain segment of the audience, it's budget and it's ability to connect emotionally with an audience. Is it a story that an audience will want to read or see or is it something that you think is off the mainstream? If you are lucky enough to get a meeting with a producer, let's change the way things are done. Connect with them as a producer would both with the emotion of your story and the intellect of your idea about how the story will fit a particular audience. Let's change the way things are done. If there are rules let's break them. I'm not suggesting that you walk into a meeting and flip the desk over and say buy my screenplay or book. But I am suggesting that you connect with a potential producer on a different level. Tell them why they can produce your work – because it is good – but also because it will be successful.

And who doesn't want to win and be successful?

Also, after you tell them what you tell them. Let them tell you what they can add. It's important for them to collaborate with you on the vision. This way they will feel ownership in it and want to see it made in the end. Let them feel comfortable with your idea as if it were their own. However, don't be a "good soldier." What I mean here is that you have to stay true to your vision even if it means being rejected. No matter what you are told, as Robert Frost aptly put it at the end of his poem "The Road Not Taken."

I shall be telling this with a sigh
Somewhere ages and ages hence:
Two roads diverged in a wood,
and I, I took the one less traveled by,
And that has made all the difference.

Be true to your journey and never sell yourself short.

Now let's get back to your script. You may be thinking, what does all of this have to do with my script and the first ten pages. Okay, let's discuss this. What does a script contain?

Let me ask it a different way, what elements are present when you write a script? Okay, Description, Action and Dialogue – let's look at these.

31

Your First Ten Pages Description, Action and Dialogue

The First Ten Pages
Description, Action and Dialogue

YOU MAY BE writing for a reader, a producer or an audience and you have got to give. And I've we stated before, that's where the ten pages come in. you have to create a hook in the beginning and once they are on board, they you can roll out any way you need to roll out. How do you get to this with character? Three ways. **Description, Action and Dialogue.** Essentially on the screen that boils down to what they do what they say, how they look, and what other characters say about them and the physical world they exist within. Your main character may say wonderful things about themselves, but they could be telling a lie. You have to show the truth. Let's talk about **DESCRIPTION.**

So, how is the best way to describe your characters in those first ten pages where your character has their initial introduction to the story? Right? So, you have to introduce them in a compelling way. In your novel you could and can take all the time you need. Went to boarding school in France, studied law – add little anecdotes. You don't have that much time and space in a screenplay. You have to cut to the chase.

INTERIOR – LIBRARY – DAY

Professor Muldoon, a crusty but benign college professor, dressed in tweed and loafers, holds an old book tightly as he hobbles down a long oak stairway into the the living room of the old English manor.

You do it all in one to three lines not a page and a half. That's it, you have to create the same impact that you would generate in a page and half description you might have in your novel. And Anthony Hopkins acts it out.

(Audience laughter)

Let's talk about that. Shall we? In your novel you have every detail covered so that you know who the characters are in every detail. Now you've got a screenplay and its all got to be in there but at around 120 pages. So you cut, but you don't want to strip everything out of it. You must capture the essence of your full character description that's in your book. What I'm saying is that you must keep the soul of your book alive and you get that 50 or 100 word description and you boil it down to five or ten words and that's the challenge. But, don't be a good soldier that writes their screenplay in 100 pages but in doing so; the end product has no life in it. You must keep the soul of your book alive and so you struggle to make sure you get in those five or ten lines of description that you don't lose any calories. It has to have the same fullness. The next element is ACTION.

Action is how your character moves in the space – the universe you have created for them. You don't have to be like "He walked slowly put one foot after another." You don't have to do that. Instead focus on something interesting about how your character does something.

Some sort of interesting action that they do like the way they tie their tie (James Bond) pet a cat (The Godfather) or walk on a sidewalk (Jack Nicholson in AS GOOD AS IT GETS). But you can create action as it happens "on the fly" as your character does it. Do you remember the old television series *Columbo (1968)?*

(Audience laughter)

I can't believe you guys remember that? Okay, well you would want to put a little bit about that character's actions in your set up. And Detective Columbo was interesting to us because we always enjoyed the way he seemed to physically fumble through each situation he was in. There was a "fumbling" almost inept quality about the character that made his adversaries not take him very seriously. They though "this guy is a total dork." But we loved to see Columbo fumble through and solve every crime despite how carefully it was planned. Sherlock Holmes is the flip side, the Victorian side. Holmes is very formal, scientific and he observes using his five sense everything intently. All his fastidious actions come into play, So action is important because it shows something about your character's way of existing physically in their universe that makes them interesting and worthy of our time. And we can go through all sorts of things to achieve that. It could be that your character in the first ten pages – their relationship with another characters shows….

(Off stage Voice)

Ten minutes? Are you sure?

(Audience laughter)

In the writing class we did yesterday, we were improvising about the "space between people." Just the space can change the way your characters react to things within their universe. You know those people in New York City on the subway? The subway car is packed – standing room only – and they are this far away from one another.)

(Catalano moves very close to a male audience member – almost touches)

(Audience laughter)

Don't worry, I won't touch you...

(Audience laughter)

Unless you want me to?

(Audience laughter.)

They are this far away and it's not a problem. Try that in Los Angeles. Try to move that close to someone and see what happens. I was on line the other day at a store (waiting to check out) and some guy (who was in a hurry) came up right behind me. He very close, I could feel him breathing on me and pressing up against my butt.

(Audience laughter)

No nothing like that... he was (I assume) trying to get the line to move faster. I turned to him and said pressing up against me is not going to make the checkout person or the line any faster. He just moved back... no comment. Now the definition of personal space in Los Angeles and now is different let's say than riding the subway in New York City during the rush hour. This guy pressing up against me in line was a violation of my personal space while it might not have even been noticeable in another situation. Definition of space in Los Angeles is different than in New York City, Tokyo or Paris. You can create visual element for your character before they even say one word. This really goes to my example of Meryl Streep in DOUBT. That kind of visual introduction says something about your character and how they move – that might take you several pages to achieve in a novel.

I recently attended a screening of the film *Chef (2014)* that (without giving anything away here) is about a chef. The opening sequence of the film (as music plays) is a series of visual shots our main character preparing food – doing the slicing, dicing – all the things a chef would do. But this action was not casual, he was preparing with a sense of purpose – so you knew right away, even before the first word of dialogue was spoken that the meal he was preparing was an important one. He wasn't just cooking breakfast for himself... it was more than that – much more. You'll have to see the film, because you're not getting anything else out of me on CHEF. Have any of you seen it?

(Audience laughter)

Really, we should stop right now and all go to the movies!

(Audience laughter)

But we can't can we? Can we? So you want to open with your characters up front and make them interesting and compelling within that first ten pages or ten minutes of screening. You want the reader/audience to want to know more about them and why they are doing what they are doing. So ACTION is very important tool for you to use to connect your characters to your audience. The other element that is important is of course DIALOGUE.

DIALOGUE is important because it is one the ways (probably one of the most important) a character communicates with an audience and other characters in your story. Dialogue is one of the primary ways your audience gets to know all the things they need to know to be connected to the story. Also, dialogue can reveal things about the character themselves; do they have a dialect, what do they say about themselves, what do they say about others, are they always telling the truth or do they lie? How do they speak? Do they speak in shortened phrases like?

(Catalano does Joe Pesci imitation from *Good Fellas (1990)*

"You said I was funny? Funny like I'm a clown, I amuse you? I make you laugh? I'm here to amuse you? What do you mean funny, funny how? How am I funny?"

(Audience laughter)

That's one way of doing it. Or does your character speak in long-winded speeches like let's say Sherlock Holmes. Figure out how what they say and how they say it fits in to what you are trying to accomplish.

You can ask my brother just one simple question and he will go off for an hour or more on it. So, really, I don't like asking him anything… you know.

(Audience laughter)

"Hey, Bro… "I call him "Bro" which is term of endearment. "How was your day?" Then he looks at me and smiles as if to say I'm so glad you asked. "Well, I got up this morning, brushed my teeth and then after that…" I think to myself… please just the highlights – do you have to tell me everything?

Is this your character? So, how they speak dialogue is just as important as exposition and content. When you finally finish the introduction of your main character, I am assuming that your main character is going to be there. Right? So your character walks in and I don't know we were doing THE SOPRANOS yesterday. I kind of dressed for it today. Your character walks in on page two and speaks for the first time with a Jersey dialect: "How ya'doin?"

(Catalano moves)

And he moves within the space leading with chin and is hunched over a bit (like he's going to whisper something important in your ear) or your main character could be an attorney with a physically that is more upright (morally driven)

(Catalano moves again this time more upright and driven.)

"How are you today?"

No chest, no chin. Little details like play strongly or should I say visually. You bring over the characteristics of your novel but with less stated. You keep your character's quality; you don't lose it with abbreviation. It's just as detailed but the detail has been compressed into Description, Action and Dialogue. Guess what? All of these elements are visual and auditory. You have moved from an intellectual medium (your novel) where everything is happens and is created in your head (your imagination) to a primarily visual medium based in external stimuli.

So, you wouldn't say your character enters leading with his chin and right foot. This type of physicality is too clinical. You might instead describe it using visual metaphors. Something like "Joey G walks in the room like a predator ready to strike with his eyes focused on the prize." The metaphor compresses it all into one short section and you can come up with a much better metaphor than I just made up on the spot.

(Audience laughter)

Then, the cinematographer, actors and directors can see it as you see it (from your words) and use their own creative input to interpret it. You might be thinking, what if they interpret my writing in a way that is different than my interpretation? Interpretation is never going to be exact. You aren't going to like this, but often the different interpretations make the impact of the work better. As we have said before, as long as the spirit of your original work is intact, you're okay. And that's what you want to set up in the first ten pages.

32

A Rose by any other name
Having the Right Title

The First Ten Pages

THERE WAS A project I was trying to get made at Warner Brothers many years ago called *Rocket Man*. It was one of those crazy projects no matter what I had in the script – everyone that heard the name wanted to see the script. It was bandied about for several years and there are even two different versions of it – one as a television series and another as a feature film. So, if was such a great title, why didn't it get put into production? Easy answer, at the same time, the Disney Company was making and released a film called *Rocketeer (1991)*, which had a lot of buzz around it but in the end was kind of a box office dud.

It's important to mention here that my *Rocket Man in* no way resembled the Disney *Rocketeer*. However, what was at one moment a title that brought interest to a project, in the next the word "rocket" in the title because it sound like "Rocketeer" brought it instant rejection. As Shakespeare said in Romeo and Juliet – "A rose by any other name would smell just as sweet."

(Audience laughter)

So, your title is important to this whole getting your work read in the first ten pages. Remember, the title is the first then they see and hear. Your title should connect with your reader on one or more of four levels of connection:

Intellectual:

The title should say something, which triggers their imagination and gives them an intellectual response such as – *12 Angry Men (1957)*, *Schindler's List (1993)*, *The Hunt for Red October (1990)*, *Inconvenient Truth (2006) or Gravity (2013)* or *Gone Girl (2014)*.

Emotional:

This title should evoke emotional response in the reader *Jaws (1975)*, *Meet the Parents (2000)*, *Life is Beautiful (1997)*, *The Notebook (2004)*, the *Hangover (2009, 2011, 2013)*, or *Fifty Shades of Grey (2015)*.

Physical:

This title should evoke a sense of immediacy and change in the reader. Want to make them physically react to what they read and perhaps do something different in their life afterward: *The Tingler (1959)*, *War of the Worlds (1953, 2005)*, *Jaws (1975)*, *Night of the Living Dead (1968)*, *JFK (1991)* or *Inconvenient Truth (2006)*.

Spiritual

This title should evoke a sense of questions in the readers mind about life and the world that they live in such as *Gandhi (1982)*, *Field of Dreams (1982)* or *Life of Pi (2012)*.

Titles can be long or short but should be clear in their connection to the reader. They should create in the reader a sense of anticipation that will drive them to open the script and begin to read it. A great title should pull them in and make them want to take the journey. Lastly, take a look at the current tile of your work and ask yourself the following questions:

1. Promise: Does your title make a promise to the reader of something that is to come? Does it fulfill a need, tell a story or explore a character? *The Exorcist (1973)*, *Gladiator (2000) or Blue Jasmine (2013)*.

2. Meaning: Is your title a literal description - *The Day the Earth Stood Still- (1951)* or is a metaphor for something else - *Snow*

	Falling Cedars – (1999)? Maybe it's a combination like *Shakespeare in Love (1999)*?
3. Audience:	Does your title speak to a specific audience? *Cinderella (1950)* focused upon children or *Cinderella Man (2005)* focused upon adults. Ask yourself what is the target audience for this idea and make sure your title speaks directly to that group. Thinking in terms of a "general audience" will get you nowhere.
4. Inevitable:	Is your title inevitable? Make your title as something they must read and can't put down – *Gone with the Wind (1939), King Kong (1933, 2005), Jaws (1975)* and any of the Godfather films (1972, 1974 and 1990). These are titles they have to read or be left out of the loop.
5. Simplicity	The shorter the better. Use terms that get their attention and call upon them to act. Make the title put them right in the middle of it all – with no other choice – *Jaws (1975), Jurassic Park (1993) or Inception (2010).*

So your title is very important because it is the gateway in which a reader or audience will enter your story. I have a lot of friends that are writers that will wake up in the middle of the night and write down what they think at that moment is a great title. They have files in Microsoft Word with just lists of titles. Titles they may never use or may rely upon at some future date when they are writing something.

(Audience laughter)

I'm not kidding. Title is very important and should be thought of your first ten pages. So we all should start keeping a list of titles that you can use when you are developing a new story. Sometimes the story may come first and then the title will go on top or at other times you can start with the title and then the story will come out of it. You can also take words out of newspaper articles, storefronts, road signs or if you feel creative graffiti.

(Audience laughter)

I was stuck on the Hollywood freeway in bumper-to-bumper traffic about a month ago when there was this piece of graffiti spray painted in red over a tattered billboard. It read: "All you need is the Right Kind of Love." Now I know the Beatles probably said it shorter and better when they sang "All you need is Love." But I thought, what an odd message to find spray-painted on a billboard sign on the freeway. So, I wrote it down.

(Audience laughter)

I may never use it… but then again you never know. So I have it tucked away in a file, like one of those athletes sitting on the bench waiting to be called into the game.

(Audience member loud sneeze)

Bless you. So your title is extremely important.

33

BEGIN AT THE END

The First Ten Pages

Okay, we have come full circle here today with this topic of writing the first ten pages of your screenplay. Now I don't want you to go after this Annual Writer's Conference and rip apart your screenplay. I want you to think about just going back to the wall.

Do you guys know who Marcel Marceau was?

(Audience member: "He was some sort of pantomime artist.")

Right. He was a mime and referred to mime as the "art of silence," and he performed professionally worldwide for over 60 years. He had a term, which loosely meant going back to the wall. This was an exercise where the mime would be placed in an imaginary box. In order to create the illusion that would have to create what was one of the most elementary mime illusions – a wall. From that point on, once the illusion was achieved the mime could move on to create a room, another person, or a larger situation. Marceau believe that no matter how advanced he had become at his art, he always went back to the wall.

What he was saying was that he went back to the most rudimentary technique in order to create his illusions. What does this have to do with your script or book.

I want you to go back to the wall. Go back to the original idea that you had before you wrote a single word. Once you have established this point, I want you to create a simple linear plot and character outline. It can be chapter-to-chapter, character driven tracking entrances and exits of your character or scene list from a screenplay.

You can do this on cards, pieces of paper or on your laptop. The important thing is that you go back to the very beginning of your story and break it down all the way to the end. Ask your self these questions:

1. What is the true ending of your story? Point of no return?
2. What is the most exciting event in your storyline?
3. What is the point in your story that your characters reach a point of no return?

If you can find these specific places in your breakdown you can begin. If you can't find them, go back to the original idea again, and rework it until these points can be clearly identified. Now here's the tricky part. Take these three points in your story and identify one point within the three that all three intersect. That is, what point in your screenplay is the true ending, most exciting and point of no return? Once you find this point, this is where your screenplay should begin.

1. Does the title of your screenplay reflect this point of no return? It should – it is your promise.
2. Set up the kind of story and characters you are sharing with the reader. Is this a comedy, a drama or horror story.
3. Let the reader know your major character. Introduce them in an interesting way. Maybe they are hanging from a cliff or falling out of an airplane.
4. Set up your story and major conflict. Give your reader an opportunity to invest in the story by raising the stakes. Maybe your main character has only 24 hours to live.

5. Lastly, do you have a message to your story and characters – Love will conquer all? Or is this just entertainment – set it up during the first ten pages.

You might be thinking, if you start your story at the very end, then there will be nothing left to tell or show the audience. I am not saying starting your story at the very end. I am saying start it at the moment just before the end. Start them at that pivotal moment where there is no point of return and your characters must go forward or perish. That's where you start, then once they are on board, you can tell and show them all the details as you go along and then give the final ending at the very last moment.

Let's go back to your promise. Start them at the most pivotal moment in your story so you create their interest. They will want to know how it all turns out. That's your job... you have to tell and show them how it will turn out. That's your promise to them. It's a promise that must be kept.

So, now let's get to work!

I want to thank you all for being such a great group. I hope you enjoy the rest of the 25th Annual Writer's Conference.

(Audience Applause)

I think we have to leave this space but I will be in the hotel lobby if any of you have questions or comments.

Thank you again.

(Audience applause)

BOOK TO SCREEN

HOW TO ADAPT YOUR NOVEL INTO A SCREENPLAY

SAN DIEGO STATE UNIVERSITY
25th Annual Writers Conference

HOW TO ADAPT YOUR NOVEL INTO A SCREENPLAY

BOOK 5

FRANK CATALANO

34

Rejection

Book to Screen

I HAVE HAD THE opportunity to be both writer and producer on different occasions and so I am familiar with how it feels to be on both sides of the table when considering screenplays for production. All stories and characters begin with an idea. Ideas can be presented to you in many forms – as a pitch, a note written on a piece of paper, a treatment, a full screenplay or a novel. No matter where you end up – what form – it all starts with an idea.

Now living in Los Angeles, you can imagine that there are a lot of people writing screenplays. Many of them are professional screenwriters but the large majority are those individuals who kind of tinker at it. They may have an idea in their head or written down and they may even have a fully written screenplay in their back pocket – but few really are writers. Who are they? They are students, bank tellers, hair stylists or teachers. In short, everybody that lives in Los Angeles (and their mother) has a screenplay or a film idea.

(Audience laughter)

The reason I am telling you this is if you have experienced rejection trying to get a screenplay read by a Hollywood producer, a lot of it has to do with the fact that there are so many people asking them to read their scripts. Getting back to what I said before, almost everyone who writes screenplays calls himself or herself a screenwriter. But the simple truth is not everyone who calls himself or herself a screenwriter actually is one. So this makes it harder to get your work read and considered.

For those of you who live in Los Angeles, next time you are waiting on line at the bank, ask aloud how many people in the bank, on line, the tellers have a screenplay. You will be shocked that almost everyone will raise their hand. So I had this thought. I have many.

(Audience laughter)

That it might be easier to get something read if it were a novel. There are fewer novelists and the work is coming through a different channel to a producer. Perhaps through a publisher, writer's agent or other representative. But here comes the rub. What if they like your novel and want to develop it into a motion picture or television show?

Your book will be assigned to a screenwriter that will take your material and create their own spin on what you have done. Then I had another thought. What if you were to have in your back pocket (if they like your book) your own version of the screen version of your book?

What is your name sir?

(Audience member: "Bill.")

What if Bill's novel is optioned by a film company and of course he's all excited about that only to find that the screenplay version radically changes his idea and story. Bill, how would you feel about that?

(Audience member: "Not very good.")

You may have an option and you might make some money but you would be locked out of the creative process. The late author Tom Clancy was furious when Paramount studios changed the ending of his novel *Patriot Games (1992)* and as a result distanced himself from the production. He of course was paid for his book but was not happy about not being in the creative process of the filmed version.

http://articles.latimes.com/1992-04-30/entertainment/ca-1996_1_patriot-games

Here's the question then. Is it a good idea to develop your own screen version of your existing novel? My answer to this question is "yes" for several reasons.

1. If your novel is published, you can draw upon its success and provide specific demographic information to a producer. This will give a potential producer an idea of how a movie of the same idea would sell. But don't stop there… movies have stars.

2. Try to attach your novel and screenplay to someone with a track record and audience following. A published book, can be sent to their agents or directly to them for consideration. If they like your book, then you can attach them to any presentation you may give to a potential producer.

3. Research talent (actors/directors) that have deals with studios. Get it to them and (if they like it) they will take it to the major studio or distributor that they have a relationship with. This is a great way to go because they have a track record and a pre existing relationship.

4. Remember that your screenplay is not your novel. It is a version of your novel that has been created for the screen. You will have to make specific choices to keep the screenplay concise and not too long. An average screenplay written in the

appropriate format is approximately one hundred and twenty pages – don't try to peddle a two hundred-page script because it will not be taken seriously.

So that was my first thought. And now for the second – our seminar description states something like BOOK TO SCREEN - "learn how to develop your novel into a marketable screenplay."

35

Know Where You Are Going – Identify Your Market

Book to Screen

Television or film including what to consider when transitioning from one medium to another. I'd like to talk about this idea today. If you are going to take your existing novel and transfer it to the film or television medium we will explore how to do that. Now it is my thinking that almost all of you sitting here today have a pre existing novel that you want to convert to a screenplay. Am I correct?

(Almost everyone raises their hands)

Great. So just about all of you have an existing novel and those that might not have an idea for one? Great. So for all of you, I want you to think about right now, what specific market your work would appeal to?

Let's take a moment and think about this. I don't want you to tell me a "general audience." I want you to be more specific. It is more focused on males or females? What age range? Any particular culture or ethnicity?

I want you to kind of put a frame around your work so that you can easily identify where it fits in to the big picture. I want you to do this, because it will have a lot to do with how you transition your existing novel into a screenplay. Remember, making movies and television is an art but it is also very much a business. So one of the first considerations your screenplay will be given is whether or not it reaches a certain market and if connecting to that market is profitable.

If I give you $50,000 and I tell you I want you to go out and buy a new car. But it just can't be any car. It has to be the safest car – one that you would put an infant in a car seat and feel okay. What kind of car would you shop for?

(Audience member: "Volvo… or Subaru…")

(Audience agreement)

How do we know that?

(Audience laughter)

Have you ever stopped to think about that? We visualize a Volvo or a Subaru because these types of cars have that position in our minds. Our brain simply states Volvo equals safe or Subaru equals safe. We know this to be so because these automobiles have been marketed to us in this manner and over time our brain has safely filed them away under "safe."

We don't have to know much more about them, just that they are safe. So what does car shopping have to do with converting your novel into a screenplay?

Answer… everything.

We want a producer or script reader or actor to think about your work in a very specific way. They will use the same process.

Your name equals novelist
Your name equals great writer

And a sub connection
Your name equals a specific genre
Your name equals a specific style

In short we want to create a position for you in the mind of a producer. The reason I am talking about this idea of creating a position is so that your work as a novelist and screenwriter is consistent, clean and to the point.

You may be thinking that you are a talented writer that has many facets to your work, many styles. All of that may be true but I want to make it as easy as possible for someone to connect to you and your work.

Think about these writers and directors – I'm just going to say names.

Woody Allen

Quentin Tarantino

Michael Bay

Or these major stars

Johnny Depp

George Clooney

Emma Stone

Meryl Streep

As I said the names, did you associate them with a kind of film or genre.

(Audience: "Yes.")

Take Woody Allen and Michael Bay – can you visualize Woody Allen directing *Transformers* (2007, 2009, 2011, 2014?)

(Audience laughter)

or Michael Bay trying to make *Midnight in Paris (2011)*, *Blue Jasmine (2013)* or *Magic in the Moonlight (2014)* like an action picture?

(Audience laughter)

I'm sure that each director would bring and interesting point of view to each picture they directed but we associate each director with a particular style of filmmaking.

So, as a writer, you want to create a framework about the kinds of things you write. You might think that I am trying to put you in a box, but it is actually quite the opposite. I want to free you within a particular framework and make it easier for individuals to connect to your work. Whether you agree or not, people like to categorize everything in their minds so that they feel comfortable and validated about what they think or feel about a particular thing.

Why not make it easier for them to do that with your work. Make your work, easier to grasp. If they want to put you in a category, let them do it. How horrible that would be to sell everything you write.

(Audience laughter)

No I'm only kidding. Once you establish a particular framework you can capitalize upon it and evolve into anything you want to be or do. What I'm talking about is not new – I'm sure you have heard it before when people say "lead with your strengths." This is a good thing.

In order to lead with your strengths, think like a marketer – who is your audience? Get to know who they are on a personal level. What do they like to eat? What do they do on vacation? What kind of car do they drive? And yes… what kinds of books, or movies or television shows to they like?

As you take this journey, a portrait of that person that is your audience will start to reveal itself to you. It will slowly emerge and when you can clearly see this person and know them as you know yourself, then you will know what to write.

So let's put a cap on this bottle… you have to know if you are selling a Volvo, a Maserati, or a Ford pickup. Each has its value and place within the universe. Don't think to yourself that you will only be the Maserati… because the Ford pickup is just as valuable in the world of ideas. Never forget that. It will make moving forward and rejection a lot less important. Speaking of rejection…

(Audience laughter)

Have you ever heard the saying "working your way to yes?"

36

WORKING YOUR WAY TO *YES*

Book to Screen

WHEN I WAS younger… much younger… I knew this guy whose name was "Mikey" short for Michael… but in Long Island, New York where I grew up… no one and I mean absolutely no one ever called you by your real name. They either called you a shorter version of your name with a "y" at the end of it.

(Audience laughter)

No this is the truth…. there were lots of Johnny's, Pauly's, Tony's and yes… Mikey's. Sometimes people put adjectives in front or in back of the name like "Big Johnny," "Little Pauly," or "Tony Maroni." In my case, I was called Frankie. But I digress.

Mikey was one of those guys who went every Friday a night to a disco in the seventies so that he could meet women for dating and other nefarious purposes. Places with names like "The Prince and the Pauper," "Mother's Lounge" and "White Brick Inn." Mikey went there to "pick up" women.

(Audience laughter)

You're probably thinking right about now that this story has nothing to do with converting your book to a screenplay. But it has everything to do with writing and selling a screenplay. It's about working your way to "yes."

What is "yes" mean anyway? It's agreement. You want someone to read and like your book or screenplay. You want them to say to you, "Yes, I will publish your work" Or "Yes, I will develop your screenplay into a film."

Am I right?

(Audience nods in agreement.)

So we all want to hear a yes at one point or another. Now, let's get back to Mikey on Friday and Saturday nights. Now, I'm going to pretend I'm Mikey – to show you what he would do. Now visualize this… he would just walk up to the first girl he saw and earnestly ask them this question:

(Catalano walks up to a woman sitting in the front row)

You want to go out with me?

(She doesn't answer then he moves to the next)

You want to go out with me?

(Audience member: "I'm married.")

(Audience laughter, Catalano goes on to the next)
You want to go out with me?

(Audience member: "No…")

(Building audience laughter)

(Catalano moves on to a young woman in the second row)

You want to go out with me?

(Audience member: "I don't think so.")

(Audience laughter builds as Catalano moves on to a woman in the third row)

You want to go out with me?

(Audience member: "Well... okay...")

Are you sure?

(Audience member: "I said okay.")

Was that a yes?

(Audience member: "I guess it was.")

Okay, then. You had me worried there for a minute.

(Audience applauds)

This is what Mikey would do every Friday night. Now each time he would ask this question, he would get some version of "No..." in response to his question... "You want to go out with me?"

Go to hell!

Not in your lifetime!

No way...

Get lost creep...

Get away from me!

And each time he was harshly turned away, Mikey would stand taller and his smile grew with each rejection. I asked him one time "You are getting shot down and humiliated every time you walk up to someone. What are you so happy about?"

He looked at me and smiled at me: "Because each time one of these babes tells me "no" I'm getting closer to "yes." And I thought at that moment, that he was crazy. But the truth was every Friday night he did eventually find someone that told him… "Yes, I will go out with you."

(Audience laughter)

So what can we learn from Mikey and how can we apply this idea to our writing.

1. **Ask the question** - This means you have to get your work out in front of people. You have to do this every day. You can set a specific number of people to talk to about your work or submit your work. Who are these people? Agents, Producers, backers in short anyone that can take your work to the next level. In Mikey's case it was "Will you go out with me?"

2. **Do not be vested in the outcome** – What does this mean? This means that you ask the question not caring whether it is a "yes" or a "no." You are asking the question just to get to "yes." If it's "no," don't evaluate it, just move on until you get to some form of agreement. Mikey just kept going forward until he got a "yes."

3. **No is only at that moment in time** – What does this mean? When someone rejects you it is only for that moment in time within the universe. If you go through an entire list of agents or producers that all reject you, then go back up to the top of the list and start all over again. Why? The moment you were rejected you were in a specific state within the universe and they were in

a specific state in the universe. Once that moment has passed, the universe has changed and the "no" you received has no meaning. There were some nights that Mikey, went through the whole bar asking his question without ever receiving a "yes." He would then start all over again and (even within the same night) people who rejected him would at a later time change their mind. Always remember, that the universe is fluid and that a "no" or a "yes" for that matter will never be constant.

4. **Always take something away with you** – What does this mean? If you are told "no" get something from the person rejecting you. In Mikey's case, he often might say something like "If you don't want to go out with me, then what about your friend?" They would tell him anything to get rid of him. "Why don't you ask her yourself?" He would reply: "Sure, what's her name?" They would always cough up the name and then he would move on to them already knowing their name with a referral from their friend. "Hello, Monica… my name is Mikey and your friend Jane just sent me over here and thought maybe you would want to go out with me." You can do the same thing with an agent who rejects you. "I really like this agency because of its reputation and size. Do you know of another agency that's just like this that might be a good fit for me?" If you ask, they will cough up a name of someone at another agency. After you get that, you contact the second agency with a note saying that you have been referred to them by the first. In this manner, you take an empty rejection and you create a situation where that rejection can spring board you to another opportunity and possibly a "yes."

5. **Visualize – What does this mean?** Form a mental image or imagine the state you would like to achieve. If you want to see your novel published or your screenplay made into a film visualize how that might appear to you and to the universe around you. This does two things – it helps you to see and know where you want to be and secondly — it makes it very clear to you what to ask for. Think of Mikey, he knew exactly what he wanted and because of that he knew what to ask for.

My last comment about working toward "Yes." I'm going to say something now that is not meant to offend anyone here today. But here goes.

Many of you sitting in this room don't truly want a "yes" with respect to your writing. Oh no! That can't be? You are all attending this writer's conference. You have spent a lot of money to travel here and even more time sitting here listening to me.

But some of you are quite comfortable to do just that. Nothing more. You really don't want to go the distance and see your work published or made into a film because you are afraid. Afraid of what?

Rejection?

Ridicule by your peers and universe?

And an even greater fear. You don't believe you know how to do it. You're afraid you can't do it at all.

And that fear is like kryptonite to Superman. It takes all the creative mojo away and leaves you empty.

I want you to think about an Eleanor Roosevelt quote:

You gain strength, courage, and confidence by each experience in which you really stop to look fear in the face. You are able to say to yourself, "I have lived through this horror. I can take the next thing that comes along." You must do the thing you think you cannot do.

Remember, "yes" is out there. All you have to do is to be open to it and allow it to come to you.

ACTING IT OUT

Improvisational Techniques for Writers
Part 2

SAN DIEGO STATE UNIVERSITY
25th Annual Writers Conference

HOW TO ADAPT YOUR NOVEL INTO A SCREENPLAY

BOOK 6

Frank Catalano

37

Using Improvisation to Develop Your Characters and Story

Acting it out

OKAY, NOW THAT we have gotten all of that out of the way. Let's talk about improvisation. What is improvisation? I mean what is your definition of it, as you understand it?

(Audience member; "When you make something up.")

What do you actually make up?

(Audience member: "You make up a character and maybe a situation and then you go with it and see where it takes you."

Right. How many of you have done improvisation before?

(Several audience members raise their hands.)

Great... tell me about what you did.

> (Audience member: "It was in college, I took a theatre class.")

What kind of class was it?

> (Audience member: "It was an acting class.")

Right. Anyone else?

> (Audience member: "I was in a comedy troupe back in Indiana. We did children's theatre type shows where we would makes stories up for small children.")

Anyone else? So the rest of you are writers and have never improvised at all before.

> (Several audience members nod in agreement.)

...and you are probably terrified of getting up here today and want to run out the door.

> (Audience laughter.)

Do not fear... this will be painless. We are going to look at improvisation as a writing tool. A writing tool to develop characters and story. Notice I said "tool" which means it's something you can use that might help you accomplish what you are trying to achieve. It will not replace whatever method you are currently using when you write.

What is improvisation? The Oxford Dictionary defines it this way:

Create and perform (music, drama, or verse) spontaneously or without preparation:
the ability to improvise operatic arias in any given style.

So that's the scary part – where it says "spontaneously – without preparation." You're sitting there and thinking – "I can't make up things on the spot – especially when a whole bunch of people are looking at me." But there's the rub. When we improvise as actors, an audience is required. But when we improvise as writers, it's an entirely different process. As writers, our end goal is to make choices about character and story within our work. Our goal is not to entertain an audience or be funny. There's a lot less pressure. Also we can start out with nothing but an idea or word or an already developed concept. So then, how do we do this?

There are two ways we can accomplish this using improvisation as a writer and I will go over both ways before we leave here today.

IMPROVISE OFF OF A DEVELOPED IDEA

One way, you may consider, is when you have a specific concept in mind. You may pick up a newspaper and read an interesting story. You would literally take that concept and put it up in an improvisation with specific characters, setting and story. From that beginning, you develop a scenario and you play it out. The persons performing within the scenario would of course provide the dialogue. What's your part? You, as the writer, through the process of selection, would choose those elements of the improvisation that would migrate to the page. Once the (more developed) concept is set on the page, you take it from there and fill in the blanks (so to speak) remain in your characters and story.

I had a specific experience with this method of writing. I did a program, one time; it was a funded grant to develop a play based upon a concept to explore spiritual love. I had an idea that was loosely based upon a poem **La Vita Nuova** (The New Life) written by Dante Alighieri in 1295. The poem is about a spiritual journey and the life long love he had for a beautiful Italian girl named Beatrice. When I wrote the grant, I explained the idea full, but there was no physical property that could be utilized to support it. So, the play had to be written from scratch. I want to add here, that an important part of the grant was to actually put this play (the one I didn't have) up on the stage. The written play and the creation of the production was the physical application of what was required for the grant. But, I had no play. All I had was the title **"Myths and Tangos"** and that the subject of this piece would be to explore the concept of spiritual love. I was asked if I had the play… and I always said yes… but that was not entirely true. Actually I had no play at all.

(Audience laughter)

So, a production date was set for a late autumn opening and this conversation was taking place in the late summer. To say the least, time was running out. So, during a family vacation, while my wife and daughters, frolicked at the beach, I sat under the shade of a palm tree and started to create a framework for this play that did not exist. I would have auditions for it upon my return from vacation and I needed some material for the actors to read. I was able to write enough over my vacation, so that I would have materials available for the actors to read at the auditions. Once the play was cast and we went into rehearsals, I had the wonderful opportunity to develop the idea on its feet with a company of actors playing out the parts as I wrote it. Each rehearsal, I would give them a rough scene to work with and they would play it out as I made notes for further development. As the actors developed the characters more fully, I began to feel more like a painter than a writer. I would watch them play the scenes and through their performances and creation of character, I would develop then next scene of the play. I was propelled in my development scene by scene. If you would have asked, what will happen next? I would have told you to come back tomorrow and watch along with me. It was very exciting. This was truly a give and take process where I took the ideas of the actors along with my concept to propel the story and characters within the play. As the rehearsals progressed, the process became more and more formal in that more elements were "set" and not changed further. The hardest part for me as a director was that the actors kept asking me when they could memorize their lines. Often I would tell them not to memorize their lines because new pages would be coming to them the next day.

I literally wrote the play as it was put on rehearsing during the day and doing rewrites at night. It was an adventure to say the least and this is one way to do it. Now, one more story.

IMPROVISE WITH NO DEVELOPED IDEA – Creating the Who, What, When and Where

One of my colleagues from NYPD Blue did an amazing project over one weekend. I asked him what he was working on and when he told me, I was astonished. He told me that he had made a movie over one weekend. I asked him, "How can you do that? What you really mean is that you shot a scene?" He smiled and replied: "No, I made a whole movie. We had six cameras and started with a single idea (it could be a word, a sentence or just an idea) and then improvised off of it. We shot the film in a chronological order shooting the whole story as it unfolds." He further explained that they wouldn't use every shot, but would utilize most of the footage. Each scene would run continuously until the director stopped it. Once stopped, they could move to another location or change the angle of the shot. Using this method of production, they shot an entire movie. In the following weeks, they edited all of the raw footage then added music and effects. It wasn't bad. When I viewed it, I was surprised that it actually had a story and characters – all of which evolve as the film progressed. So in this specific example, the creators started out with literally nothing. Then utilizing the actors developed a full story (who, what, when, where, why) and just went with it. The script came after the film in that case. Once the footage was shot and edited, a script was created. In my particular case, writing my play, this method of creation enabled me to develop each scene in a way that I had never done before – it engaged all of my senses as I watched and listened to the actors (as the characters) go through each scene. So we will look at this today, how do we develop a script out of an idea or how can we develop something out of nothing?

Okay, but here's the question. How do you know what your making up is any good? How do you know if it even fits what you are trying to accomplish? How can we collectively discover what kind of improvisational approach will help you create compelling story lines, vibrant characters and realistic dialogue? So, what kind of techniques can you employ? There are certain frameworks and exercises you can do either on your own or in this public setting. So, today, we will take a look at that.

Lastly, we will do some actual exercises together where I will give you a premise, a line, a character or nothing. Together we can see what you come up with using these techniques. I know I've asked this… but really… how many of you have improvised before? Okay, more than a few, this will be a fun group.

(Audience laughter)

BEING FUNNY

For those experienced improvisers here today, did you ever feel the pressure that you had to be funny when you improvised?

(Several audience members raise their hands)

All right, we will let that practice go right out the door. We don't have to be funny. All we have to do is play the scene we are in. You don't have to enter in a contest of "who can say the funniest one liner" in each scene. All you have to do is play one moment that will lead into the next and so forth. Just react to what you are given and move the scene forward. We don't want to play the high pressure "I can be funnier than you" contest because when that occurs the plot and characters suffer. Also, in a workshop situation, like we have today, a normal person – one that is not adept at saying funny quips every thirty seconds is going to refrain from wanting to improvise. They will feel that they are not funny and will hang back. This is a way we do not want to go. We are writers here and the goal is to develop characters and a story – not just to be funny. If your story turns out to be humorous, than that's great. But your story and characters could also be living within a dramatic situation that is not funny. So, I am not saying you shouldn't be funny here today. What I am saying is that the most important thing you can do here today is play the scene, listen to what is said and react to what is done. Let your story and characters evolve out of that situation rather than a series of one-line jokes. We want the stories and characters that are inside of you to come out! Some of you here today, may have a story inside of you, that you aren't even aware of… it's just sitting there inside you… just below the surface or in your subconscious just waiting to be created. So we definitely want to discuss how to avoid the "improvisation has to be funny" syndrome. If you want to be funny… be funny. But you don't have to be funny.

Now, why would we want to use improvisation for the creation of a new story or let's say an existing manuscript? What do you think?

(Audience members: "Fresh Ideas… A new way to look at your story…")

Yes?

(Audience members: "With improvisation, you don't have to follow certain rules.
You can do anything you want.")

Yes, like in the last seminar that we shared together – you know the thing about the page ten… you are obsessed with getting in all in during the first ten pages and suddenly you do an improvisation and it doesn't follow any of those rules or have any of those expectations and guess what? It's good!

And other times you improvise and it doesn't fit, it's not so good and you explore another way of doing it. So, improvisation helps us explore. On a very rudimentary level it helps us listen to our character's dialogue. Last session we talked about a slang or particular vernacular for a character or a voice that made it come to life. So even if you have something written down on a page and you improvise off of off that page, it can take that character to a place that you perhaps would not have thought of (in a good way). By listening you get an understanding of the sounds of the character… what they say, if they repeat themselves and whether or not that is effective. Chemistry is also important, improvisation helps us listen and watch our characters interact with other characters with your story. That's something I want to try today. Two different people come together in a space. Are they a perfect fit? Are they opposites? Which works better for your story? What happens when you get two opposites and put them in a room together? That could be your idea about what you are going into? What if we had a Catholic priest and an atheist stranded on a deserted island? How would that play out? This type of exercise would help a writer discover the meaning in a scene. It might be funny, but that's not why we would explore it. We want the meaning and so we explore if off the page. Now, I have another question… how many of you have screenplays already written or are you all novelists?

(Audience response – raising their hands)

Okay, we've got a couple… and what about novelists? How many of you have existing novels that you want to adapt into a screenplay?

(Larger audience response raising their hands)

Okay, then most of you are novelists. So this is for all of you… have you ever been in a situation when someone says to you, "What's your book about?" "What's your screenplay about?" Now you wrote it so you have to answer it right?

(Audience laughter)

You can't say I don't know. And you can't say – "guy gets up in the morning and so on…" and you tell them the plot. No they don't want to know that. They want to know what your novel or screenplay is about… they don't want you to tell them the story. Do you see the difference? So, how did you answer that question?

(Audience response)

Did you tell them your story… or that you didn't know what it was about or both?

(Audience member: "Both.")

Both? Sometimes we create things… but when asked that simple question, we cannot answer it. Sometimes, we have no idea what our story is about. We just wrote it… but don't ask what it is all about. You will have to read it to answer that question.

(Audience laughter)

In fairness to you and every other writer in this hotel today, you might be asked to write a segment of a creative idea and not really know what the whole concept is about. Television is often that way. You only know what you are writing within your particular episode but have a much lesser understanding of the total framework of the television program. They may ask you for a particular outcome within a certain page count… and you start off with that end game in mind and sort of back your way into it. I once had to write about two minutes of dialogue for existing footage of a horse race that was playing on an overhead television in an off track-betting parlor. Now the television hung prominently over the heads of two other characters that were talking about committing a crime, but the horse race had to also be in the space because it was on camera for the whole scene. To make matters worse, specific things had to be written to connect to what was on the screen and then as the scene ended the horses starting off the line in a race… all this and a crime being committed in the foreground of the shot. All I had to concern myself with was the horse race and had to make sure there were sufficient spaces in my dialogue so that the scene below the television set could play out. In my scenario, I didn't have to know what it meant. All I had to be concerned with was the scene below the television in the shot and the total run time. All of that had to fit together. So, I created my own universe of the horse race with names or horses, owners and jockey's that played out underneath the scene in the betting parlor. To get to that point, I relied on improvisational techniques.

38

IMPROVISATION AS A CREATIVE JOURNEY

Acting it out

IMPROVISATION IS MORE of a journey. Why do I say journey? I think of a journey as going from one place to the other where you encounter different things and people. Like an actual journey, sometimes your characters will wander off your plot path and you will have to struggle to bring them back. Improvisation is a way of illustrating the journey and showing it to you so that you can make those choices. Sometimes you can read something multiple times and you don't understand it and then you see it up on its feet or hear it and it all falls into place. Why? Because you are engaging all of your senses (sight, touch, smell, taste and hearing) and so you experience your work on a totally different level. You are not just playing it all in your brain and imagination – you are up on your feet acting it out. And because you are exploring, things can happen by accident that are good.

Here's the deal. Ultimately, you can experience the idea, your characters or story off the page utilizing all of your senses. Now I will digress. Not all of our senses are bestowed to us equally. Some of us are "visual" people – meaning they remember and respond to almost all of what they see. Some are "auditory" people – meaning they remember and respond to almost all of what they hear... and touch, taste and smell and so on. Some of us are "touch/feel" people – almost all the Italians in the house.

(Audience laughter)

Some are odor driven... we react mostly to smell. Or there may be a few "tasters" out there.

(Audience laughter)

So, improvisation engages everything and that why we experience our work in a totally way. Now when you write, in front of your computer or legal pad, we engage all of those things through our imagination. However, improvisation is really a hands on method that breaks the preconceived responses that we may harbor in our imaginations. It allows us to look at our work from a totally different perspective. Probably, the perspective that is the closest to the audience way of looking at your work that you will ever get. When you sit and write your books, it is very difficult for you to be, to sound like, and to feel all the things your characters experience. With improvisation, you experience it, just as an audience would. Therefore, you will have a better understanding of your work's meaning. If the meaning of your work is clear to you, it will be clear to an audience because you are experiencing in a similar way. So that's one reason to use improvisation.

Now, in my own writing, I have written many plays for theatre, screenplays, animation and of course books. My roots are firmly in the theatre, so I often have a live reading of my work either on stage or a table read. This is something I always do, for almost all of my work. You can do this as well by renting a small theatre for an evening or using your living room. You cast as you would if you were doing it and then at the reading you can just sit back and listen to what you have written. On certain occasions for certain projects, I also do a staged reading which is kind of a combination of reading and stage version.

What I'm saying is that a staged reading for me includes movement. I may set the actors up in a semicircle on the stage and have them get up and go to the center of that semicircle when the read their scenes. If you choose a staged reading format, you should probably have at least one-maybe two rehearsals so that everyone knows where they have to be and what they have to do during the reading. I often put actors playing characters that have a lot of scenes together next to one another. They still have to get up to read or sometimes they can do their scene from where they sit. I like this because, getting up, allows the actors to physicalize the reading. In this manner, you get a sense of how the words you have written translate into the physical world. I just like to watch and listen... I rarely take notes. I just want to watch and listen just as if I were sitting in an audience. I don't want my face buried in the manuscript writing notes. I just want to experience the work as it was meant to be. However, I often ask the actors and audience to make notes and when we discuss the reading afterward, certain elements may come to the surface. I take a lot of notes during the discussion part of the reading. If you do decide to have a reading, listen to what is being said. Don't be defensive if you are criticized. Just write whatever you feel is important to your characters and story. You will also invariably get comments on typos or grammar you may choose to accept or ignore. So a live reading of your manuscript is another way to get your work up on its feet so that you may experience it with all of your senses. Improvisation is also a great tool to get around writer's block. How many of you have ever experienced writer's block?

(Audience reaction – several hands go up in agreement)

Right. Well using improvisation is a great way to break through the creative barriers imposed by writer's block. Of course when you put your work up on its feet and use actors upon a stage or your living room, you must be open to their interpretation. Often I have found that readings by actors improve the presentation and my understanding of the work... and yes, once in a while, I have had readings where I was not happy with one or two actors interpretation of my characters. But remember, once you put your work on its feet, it becomes a collaborative experience. You are no longer writing in your head, and different creative values of actors and an audience my change the outcome of how your work is presented. My advice is not to take notes on performances, just sit back and experience your work. When it's over, walk away from it along with an audience with a sense of what you and the audience thought the work was about. So, let's explore the question a little more. How can the use of improvisation assist a writer (of fiction or screenplays) in the development of character and story? Or What if you have no story? Nothing? How many of you have been to the hairdresser, the barber, a lawyer or the grocery store? We all have and they will tell you… "Why don't you write a story about a (fill in the blank) a hairdresser, a lawyer, a grocery clerk?" My answer is, there is no story… and they'll answer, "You know the funny stuff that happens."

That is still not a story.

(Audience laughter)

The funny stuff that happens is not a story. You can't write that story because it lacks fully developed characters and a plot. But you could utilize improvisation to develop perhaps an aspect of such a set up. Once someone gave me an idea to do a story about a person's diary and I said "what about it?" The idea was that someone would find a diary and that contained in that diary was a story… an unanswered mystery. I kept on asking, "What was the story?" They shook their head and said, "I don't know… it's in the diary?"

(Audience laughter)

Then I thought, what if I improvise a story around a diary? Do a set up where a New York City detective arrives at a crime scene that contains the skeleton of a little girl buried in a wall. What makes it different is that the remains have been buried there for what looks like twenty years. There isn't a clue to who the little girl is except for the remnants of the dress she wore and that by her side, the detective also finds a hand written diary. The last faded entry was written just moments before she was murdered. The faded notation partially describes her killer. Now we improvise off of that and now we are starting to get a story. The characters begin to evolve and the story starts to fall into place.

But sometimes and idea is just that. You try to improvise this concept but don't get any traction. Characters do not reveal themselves and the idea remains just an idea. Despite your writing and improvisation it never matures to the next level. Sometimes that happens, and that is okay. You just take it, put it on the back burner and maybe sometime in the future it will mature or you will link it with another idea and it will start to evolve.

39

Improvisation as a Creative Tool

Acting it out

IMPROVISATION CAN BE used as a creative writing tool and not necessarily a thing you have to worry about for performance... and you don't have to worry about being funny. And you need to give and take... that means letting it flow. Don't become locked into one specific idea. If we do an improvisation and Bill

(Catalano points to audience member)

And... what's your name?

(Audience member: "Jennifer.")

Okay, what I am about to describe is an example. Bill and Jennifer. I'm not going to give you anything but a word...

(Audience member Bill: "Cool.")

And then I'll say to the class, "Someone give me a word."

And one of you will say, "Apple!"

Then Bill and Jennifer begin an improvisation... I'm not actually saying you are going to do this... I'm just using you for my fictitious example.

(Audience laughter)

Then Bill gets started and does a whole thing about an apple.

"Look at this apple... this is a special apple... I wonder if it's sweet?"

And the entire improvisation becomes a literal discussion based upon the word that was given. Apple.

Now the problem with my example is that the entire improvisation is wrapped around the discussion about an apple. Why? Because the first word I provided was "apple." What's wrong with this fictional example? By focusing on the just the word "apple," we close out all other possibilities.

Instead, what I want you to think about is not just doing a literal interpretation of the word or idea but instead taking that idea or word and transforming it into something entirely different. Use "apple" or whatever your idea or word is a springboard into an entirely different meaning. Something like:

"Look at this apple it's a strange color... it came from that tree over there by the barn. There were strange lights and sounds coming from that barn last night...

Did you see those lights?

No, but I did see a light in the sky… about midnight. The light I saw hovered over the apple tree for about an hour. It was a strange colored glowing light.

We took apple and made it a story about a possible UFO… sighting. We took the concept and went on a journey, not knowing where it would lead us. It becomes something else that can be more interesting than just talking about the apple itself.

Many people, because of television and the Internet tend to literalize everything they encounter. Computers and the Internet facilitate that. You type or say a phrase and you literally get all ramifications of that phrase. They type in "apple" and they get the literal understanding of Apple in our modern culture – a fruit or a computer company. No UFO's on the horizon here. **Remember this, an apple doesn't just have to be an apple… it can be a reason to start on a journey.** Just allow it to crawl out of the pond and be what it wants to be.

(Audience member: "Are we going to have to get up and improvise.")

Yes, we are.

(Audience member: "I already did some improvisations yesterday.")

Well, you are going to do a few more today. Just a few.

(Audience laughter)

Nothing too crazy… remember this is a writer's workshop. I don't want to frighten anyone.

(Audience laughter)

Catalano cartoon voice: "Oh no! They're doing improvs! I'm gone!"

(Audience laughter)

So, don't be literal and we will do an exercise to help us with that. Don't worry, when we do the exercise I won't ask you to play a slice of bacon sizzling on the pan. Nothing like that. But I want you to start thinking about starting with a physical activity.

(Audience laughter)

40

USING PHYSICALITY TO CREATE CHARACTERS AND TELL YOUR STORY

Acting it out

WHEN WE COMMUNICATE ideas or who we are in life we don't only use words, we also use physicality to convey our meaning. So, as you write, it's not only about what your character speaks, it is also about what they physically do within a given space. One of the major barriers to improvisation, is many individuals have a hard time figuring out what to say. What I'm telling you here, is that you don't have to say anything. You can create a character and place them in an environment and just let them react physically to that environment. Our characters, as in life, react physically in a different way, to each environment they find themselves within. For example, your physicality might be different if you are sitting in a doctor's office waiting for test results, or walking down a dark alley in the middle of the night or climbing the bleachers at a rodeo show. How a character reacts physically or moves physically within an environment can tell us a lot about who they are and their emotional state.

In a given improvisational situation, don't worry too much about making up things to say. Instead, you can communicate within an improvisation by just using your body language. Also, there are those instances where the dialogue and the physicality are not in agreement. The script might say one thing with dialogue but mean another with physicality. Here let's do an improvisation right now.

(Catalano selects an audience member to participate)

Your line is "How are you?" and my line will be "fine." Okay? Now we will do this for real, and I will say my line but I will use physicality to communicate what is really happening. Ready?

(Audience member: "Yes.")

Okay…

(Audience member: "How are you doing?")

(Catalano assumes a negative physicality with his arms tightly folded)

Fine…

All right, so the reality is something quite different than the lines would otherwise indicate. You are asking me if I am fine. I say yes, but really I am not fine. The character I have created is actually angry or at least concerned. Now let's try it again.

(Audience member: "How are you doing?")

(Catalano smiles and assumes an open physicality)

Fine! It says, "fine" so I am going to be fine!

(Audience laughter)

Here now we have the exact opposite situation. We can use physicality and without even talking we can convey the meaning of the scene. So within your improvisation, some of your characters may not speak very much or perhaps not speak at all. Let's say in your novel you have written about a painter… you know a painter that paints on a canvass… not a house painter.

(Audience laughter)

… and in a given scene they are painting but they are also – let's say angry – so you have an older man (an artist) paint angrily. He splashes paint upon the canvass and maybe uses jabs instead of smooth brush strokes. All of these actions convey the emotion of the character within the scene, but a line has not yet been spoken. On the other part of the stage or shot, a young female sits quietly and content reading a book. Both characters are in the same room, but don't look at each other. That's your opening scene as the camera starts to roll or the curtain goes up in the theatre. Immediately the audience watching will understand the emotional content of the scene even if the characters haven't spoken a word. What would the dialogue add to the scene? Well, maybe we could find out why there is anger? Maybe the male character painting is jealous of the female character because she has been out all night. How would you know this… perhaps through dialogue when they finally start to speak?

Female: Will you paint me today?

Male Painter: Yes… I'm just changing something here.

Female: When?

Male Painter: When I'm ready.

Female: Should I take my robe off and get on the couch?

Male Painter: You're quick to do that. You like taking off our clothes.

> Female: Just trying to help… move it along.
>
> Male Painter: You got back late last night… you thought I was sleeping… I wasn't.
>
> Female: (flips the magazine page) Interesting article about Spain…
>
> Male Painter: It was very late… you've been drinking with Raul again?
>
> Female: They are discouraging bull fighting… did you know that?
>
> (The painter jabs his brush harshly into the canvas she turns the page of the magazine.)

Now as the story unfolds we start to have an idea about what's going on. However, it's not just the dialogue that tells us… it's the physicality of the characters as well. You can convey all of this using improvisation – letting it all take its path and then taking what you have discovered back to the page. Use improvisation as a tool and don't be literal. Television kills us. They have to tell their story (if it's an hour long show) in forty-three or forty four minutes and it all has to fit within a very specific format. Not a lot of room for exploration.

> (Audience member has a question: "In writing the script, you have already talked about not writing it as if you are the director or including very specific camera angles.")

Yes…

> (Audience member continues: "So the actors should act and the directors direct.")

Yes…

Audience member: ("So, when you're writing that script and you have in your mind's eye how that scene is going to look – how do you get that element of your ideas on the page? Is there a happy medium?")

Yes, there can be a happy medium. What Bill is talking about we discussed in yesterday's workshop. The economy of words... using your words to obtain the greatest impact. You want to let the actors and the director know how the scene will look and what's going on but don't tell them how to act it or how each camera angle should be set up. Remember, that film and theatre are collaborative arts. Everybody gets to provide creative input. As a writer, you have the challenge of giving them as much as it takes to know what is going on but not so much that you are intrusive. Let's look at what you have to work with in a script?

41

Page to Screen - Description Action and Dialogue

Acting it out

THE THREE ELEMENTS I'm talking about are description, action and dialogue. Let's look at them.

DESRIPTION: The depiction of the physical universe that your characters live in.

ACTION: How your characters move within the universe that you have created.

DIALOGUE: What your characters say about themselves, other characters, their situation and the universe the move within.

Now when you are working within the literary medium, you can take all the time and all the words you need to describe to the reader about your character and what is going on in your narrative. The words you use are directly aimed at creating the idea in your imagination in the reader's imagination. It's a one on one relationship. When you move over to scriptwriting, you are now describing what is in your imagination to any number of people (producers, directors, scene designers, costume designers, actors) with the tacit understanding that these individuals will add their own interpretation to what you have created. So, think of your three elements **description, action and dialogue** as a starting point (not and ending point). You have to give them just enough to understand your vision, but leave them enough room to add their own. And that is why in screenwriting, we cut to the chase quickly. We use our words with a sense of economy. Adding all sorts of intricate camera angles is for example is not a good idea because it limits the Director of Photography's creative participation in the film. Just give them enough so that they know what's going on and then they will add their piece to the creation.

Take the example we just went through with the older male painter and his young female lover. Do we describe that scene with an entire paragraph? No. Just a couple of lines which will give who ever is reading it a clear cut idea of what scene should look like, who the characters are and what is going on.

INT. ARTISTS STUDIO – DAY

John looking worn and disheveled from sleeping in his clothes the night before jabs his brush into the canvass Julia naked except for a thin robe waits to begin her sitting. His brush strokes are agitated and jagged as she quietly turns the pages of a magazine.

Now I just made that up and it probably should have more economy of word and also include a bit of description for the studio. You shouldn't do an extensive description of the scene and then explain in detail what's going on in each characters mind as live out the scene. The characters through action and dialogue will do that for you. If you get too specific, you will lose the reader.

John using magenta #17 spills the oil on his new shoes he had specially shipped from Italy. As he move to clean them, the paint splattered even more and spread on his red and tan all wool carpet which he purchased on his last trip to Bangladesh. The camera pans slowly up John's shoe to his right corduroy pant leg now spattered with paint up to his unshaven face and open shirt and Ralph Lauren tie.

(Audience laughter)

This might work in the literary medium but long-winded description and detailed camera angles and director's notes won't work in a screenplay. The dog won't hunt. You have got the let everyone have a creative piece within the puzzle. Theatre and film are by their very nature collaborative arts. Now getting back to improvisation.

It's okay to sometimes play the "opposite" within a given improvisation. Assuming that an improvisation, in your case is a scene from your book... you can from time to time make the physicality and the dialogue *contrast* one another. What I mean here is... that the dialogue might say one thing but the physicality says something quite different. This is a similar approach to the example we just did a moment ago.

For example, if I said to you that I was going to beat you to a pulp.

(Catalano looks at one man in the audience.)

I don't really mean that... I mean if we were improvising and I said that I was going to beat you to a pulp but my physical gestures were the opposite. I keep saying that I will beat you to a pulp but I keep backing away from you. This is an example of contrasting the physicality with the dialogue. So if you get tossed into an improvisation and the situation that is given to you is "you're are breaking up with your girlfriend... go!" You don't have to cut to the immediate chase, "I'm leaving you! It's just not working out!"

Instead, you can try the opposite:

"Hi honey, sorry I'm late."

Now you do something very strange – you tie your shoe and now you intently look at your shoe as you tie the lace very slowly.

"I'm really sorry I'm late. I had to work late at the office... and it looks like I'm going to be doing this every night. I was thinking...

Still focusing on the shoelace.

... that we should take a break from one another for a while.

The shoe is tied.

I need to make some money now so I can get out of debt. It's really not you... it's me."

Suddenly the guy's shoe is the most important thing to him. Why? So he can hide there. He can focus his energy on the shoe rather than looking his girlfriend in the eye. Why can't he look her in the eye? It could be any number of reasons—but probably because he is not telling the truth. It's actually called "creative hiding" and is a great way to tell if someone is not telling you the truth. Please don't try this at home without supervision.

(Audience laughter)

Guys here... don't do the shoe now... because they know it.

(Audience laughter)

It could be anything to take the focus off of you. It could be the moon in the sky, a spot on the wall or (a little more risky) focus on a body part. When they ask you a question, you can say before you answer:

"Your hair... it looks great. Did you get it done today... it looks really great."

(Audience laughter)

So even though the purpose or outcome of the scene is to break up... you play the opposite but you still complete the objective. What about listening?

So improvisation, should not be literal – you can and should take whatever idea you begin with and then let it evolve on its own. Also, don't forget physicality is a great way to create character and situation. You can go a long way in creating story and character without ever saying a word. But I also want you think again about the "spontaneous" part of the definition. You have to create elements of character and story on the spot. To do that you have to be a good... no a great listener.

Being a great listener when doing an improvisation is essential. If another actor gives you something within an improvisation you have to acknowledge it. If they say they were late because the trolley was late... don't reply and say all the planes were late at the airport.

This tells the audience that you are not listening to what's going on. Also, listen to what your characters say about themselves and what other characters say about them. Sometimes characters like people don't tell the truth. That can also be revealing. There may be some "code" words imbedded within what the characters say. For example, we all know that our parents love us and when we see them, no matter how old we are, they still look at us at their child. They can say one word to us (that's a code word) and suddenly we are ten years old all over again.

(Audience laughter)

Or pre set patterns.

Catalano: Hi Mom, how are you?

Mom: Just sitting here ***alone*** like a dog.

Catalano: A dog?

Mom: Yes, **alone** just like a dog… an **abandoned** dog.

Catalano: Alone?

Mom: Like a dog…

Catalano: What are you doing?

Mom: **Waiting.**

Catalano: **Waiting** for what?

Mom: **Waiting** to die.

Catalano: Why is that?

Mom: Because you never call…

Catalano: Mom, I call you every day… I just called you yesterday!

(Audience laughter)

You can use these kinds of pre set patterns or code words within a given improvisation.

Accept what you are given (whatever the reality is) within a given improvisation. This is an acting note as much as it is a writing note. If two characters step into a space and it goes something like this:

Character 1:   Good morning.

Character 2:   Morning.

Character 1:   Nice day…

Character 2:	I guess.
Character 1:	Could you push the 14th floor for me please?
Character 2:	14? I don't know what you're talking about – there are no buttons here…we're on a bus stop!

In this case where are they?

(Audience – "On an elevator.")

How do we know that?

(Audience – "Their physicality – the way they are standing.")

(Audience - "He asked him to press an elevator button.")

Right, but character #2, decided to create their own reality and violated the reality set up by character #1. Here's another example.

Character 1:	I'm sick and tired of cleaning up after you. You always leave your socks on the floor. I'm out of here!
Character 2:	Excuse me? Is that paper or plastic or did you bring your own bags?

(Audience laughter)

You may get that once in a while… and what you can do is try to bring it back to the original reality or go with the new reality. But there needs to be only one reality or the audience will get confused.

Character 1:	I'm sick and tired of cleaning up after you. You always leave your socks on the floor. I'm out of here!

Character 2: Excuse me? Is that paper or plastic or did you bring your own bags?

Character 1: Very funny… I'll take plastic… and while you're at it… throw out the garbage.

Character 2: Okay…

Character 1: This is the last time I'm doing this. Clean up after yourself!

The whole idea about improvisation and even writing for that matter is to "give and take." Especially if you are writing characters and you are in the zone – you have no idea what will come out of your character's mouths. So whatever they say, you should listen to it and somehow react. Otherwise, why is it written for someone to read? If it's not important, doesn't help your story evolve and further develop your character, why should a reader or an audience sitting in a theatre bother to listen to it? You can have your characters "not listen" to one another but whatever they say should be of interest to an audience.

42

LET YOUR CHARACTERS EXPERIENCE YOUR STORY THROUGH THEIR FIVE SENSES

Acting it out

WE ARE ALL people who experience the world (our characters are the same way) through our five senses – sight, touch, taste, smell and hearing. You might be writing characters with six senses – that can see dead people or aliens...

(Audience laughter)

I'm saying for most of us, five senses. But our senses are not all the same are they? Think about this as a hot spot for a character that they can use one of their senses more because they are better at it. They could be "visual" so that they react to and remember everything the see in vivid detail. They could be "auditory" where they react more effectively to everything they hear. We have talked about his in other workshops. Think about this kind of attribute, if your character is not working for you. You feel they are cliché' or an off the shelf grocery store type of character. Change they way they perceive their universe through one of their senses. Try that and see what happens to them and your story. You could also improvise off of this concept.

> Character 1: You never tell me that you love me…
>
> Character 2: What are you talking about? I washed your car yesterday…look at it!

Character #1 is auditory – they need to hear the words I love you. Character #2 is visual – washing the car is a visual way of saying I love you.

> Character 2: I love you baby…
>
> Character 1: Don't tell me you love me… show me! Stop going out drinking with your friends every night.

Character #2 is auditory – they are telling them something they think they want to hear.

Character #1 is visual – they want to see something happen.

How does your character perceive their universe? Utilize an improvisation to illustrate the best way to show it. If you think about characters such as Sherlock Holmes – his whole thing was observation. I'm not saying he wasn't an auditory person as well. But his major quality was to utilize visual observation to deduce the reality of the situation.

Holmes says in *A Scandal in Bohemia*: **"You see, but you do not observe. The distinction is s clear."** He reacts to the world around him intellectually, emotionally, physically and spiritually using his five senses. But, I would think his visual sense leads the way. Notice I also mentioned three words intellectual, emotional and physical. What's that?

Think about when you are telling a story and your characters enter into it at various points of the narrative. Now we have talked about their sensory strengths and weakness. But what is your character's state of being within the narrative that you have created? Let's define this by the three terms I just mentioned.

Intellectually: This is your character's mental state. What do they think about the universe they live in? What is their place in it? What is their intellectual opinion about a given topic? Are they Republican or Democrat or anarchist? What do your characters think about things?

Emotionally: This is self-explanatory. How do they feel about the universe this live in? What is their emotional state within their universe or moment we see them in? If they were on vacation and sitting on the water's edge on a beautiful tropical island what would their emotional state be? A moment later, a tsunami alarm goes off and they see tidal wave heading toward the beach they are sitting on – what is their emotional state then?

Physically: Again, this is self-explanatory. How doe your character physically interact with the universe you have provided for them. What is their physical state? The physical state of a character can be different within certain cultural settings. For example, we discussed Sherlock Holmes who lived during the Victorian era. What was the physical norm then? How is it different then now? Perhaps the physical state of a character might be different from culture to culture. Their physical state might be different in India than in Japan.

Spiritually: Lastly, how do their core beliefs about the nature of their universe govern the way the move through it, think about it and feel about it. Their core beliefs act as a framework for the other three. Often in stories, the spiritual nature of a character changes as they progress through the story. The characters evolve as the story progresses.

Now that we have discussed how your characters perceive their universe, let's look at ways to assign specific attributes to each character – that can help us and an audience define who they are.

43

Developing Character - The Three "P's"

Acting it out

IMPROVISATION CAN HELP us discover *then* show all of these character elements. So ask yourself, where your characters fall within these four areas. Also on a more elementary level, when a reader or audience member first meets your character within your work, it's like meeting a person for the first time. The audience wants to know something about them, so they can comfortably follow them through the rest of your narrative. Within your improvisation, when we say find the Who, What, When, Where and Why… this would be the "who." What is the sub set of "Who" that you could communicate clearly to your reader or audience? What does the "who" actually mean? We could be simplistic and say our character is an astronaut in space. But is that enough to grab the reader's or audience attention? Think of it this way, when you meet a new person at a party or dinner – what are the things you often want to know so that you can then start a conversation? Also, by extension, you want to know these things so that you can make a decision to continue the conversation or move on to another person. Here they are:

Professional:

We all want to know what the person does. Are they a student, an astronaut, a soldier or doctor? Also, where and how do they exercise this professional description? If someone tells you they are a writer, but they haven't published or produced anything you might think that they are not a writer. When someone in Hollywood, says they are an actor, you invariably ask them what they did. Knowing they are an actor is not enough – you want to know more. My wife once met the late actor Donald O'Conner – the actor who played the scarecrow in the Wizard of Oz what he did as his profession. We met at a party and he said to my wife:

    O'Connor: Hello, I'm Donald O'Connor

    Wife: Hello Donald! Please to meet you. So, Donald what do you do?

    So we always want to know more when we meet someone for the first time. We want to know what they do. Why? Because it tells us something about who they are and whether or not we want to know more about them. We may not ask them outright as soon as we say hello but eventually we get around to it. Do you agree?

    (Audience member: "Yes...")

Personal:

The second thing we all want to know when we first meet someone is his or her personal state or situation. Are they married, single, in a relationship, not in a relationship, divorced, straight, gay, widowed and we find this out through the conversation. Think of the character Mel Gibson played in *Lethal Weapon (1987)* - he was widowed but in a very violent way. We learn that he had lost his whole family. We don't expect them to say: "Hello, I'm Mel and my family was murdered. We find these things out through conversation. But we still want to know. Why? Because we color everything they do or say through their personal state or situation. There are no blanket rules here but we want to put the people we meet in a box and define them in a way that we can understand. Characters are people and while we want to write complex characters, we have to give the audience something that they can hold onto. As you evolved your story and characters, you can further define their personal state so that each character is unique.

Private:
This one is really a process of deduction and can be something only your character knows. Maybe they are considered a "war hero" but really they are a coward. It is some deeply held private element of your character that they want to keep unknown. It's their secret that the audience may know at the start but it is not apparent to other characters in your story. If the audience, does not know this secret about them at the start it should be revealed as the story progresses or at the ending.

So these three P's become part of the "Who" you create within an improvisation. You might not want to do all three at once within a short improvisation, but these three P's could be a useful tool to develop your character within several improvised scenarios. The overall goal is to develop multifaceted characters that have many levels rather than one-dimensional stereotypes. Even if you don't have a lot of time to develop your character, make choices about selecting certain elements to develop.

Lastly, I want to say this about improvisation – have fun!

Now when I say have fun, it really sounds like a very cliché statement. But what I really mean is to find the joy in the creative process. Creating anything, can sometimes be very frustrating because we have a certain idea in mind and when we try to take that idea a put it to paper, it somehow loses something. Improvisation is all about, letting things flow and then selecting out what is created what will work for your idea. I know it's very hard for some of you to just let go and see where your characters and story will take you. But if you will let that happen you will discover things that are within you that you don't even know exist. Not every idea you have is going to be great. A lot of your ideas might just be okay and then some of them might be awful. But that's where we come in, we let the creative juices flow and then select only those ideas that work for us. Find the joy in this... let it be a place you go to over an over again to explore. So let's try some?

(Audience laughter)

Are we allowed to mess this room up a little bit? I just want to move the seats out this way so we can make a circle. I won't ask you to sizzle like a piece of bacon or bark like a dog... so don't worry. Right about now, you're saying to yourself: "Where's the door... I'm a writer not an actor... why did I sign up for this?"

(Audience laughter)

"I could have been in the agents seminar."

(Audience laughter as they move chairs)

Okay... excellent... just as long as we can a nice round circle to work in. Does anyone have a problem standing for a few minutes?

(Audience reply: "No.")

You mean I have to stand? I'm outta here! Okay, there's a lot of us... so we will have to squeeze this circle a bit... but we'll get it done. This is the closest thing (we are about to do) to being a piece of sizzling bacon... and then that's it. I am going to tell you why we are doing it... what we are about to do is an exercise in accepting what you receive in an improvisation. No matter what you get, you will have to use it as given to you. Some of you are going to see this coming around the circle toward you and think that you have a wonderful idea and then before it gets to you, someone else has done what you thought of. Once that happens, you have to come up with something else. No repeats... this is quick and easy without any dialogue. What I have in my hand is an ordinary pen. What I am going to do is make this pen into something. It can be the total object or just a part of it... a handle or something like that of a much larger object. Okay? What I am asking you to do is take this object and create something out of it other than a pen. We will start with me... I am going to make something out this pen, and use it. Then, I'm going to pass it to my left and you will take what I have made, use it... then make something else out of it and pass it to your left. If you don't know what I am handing you, give it back and make me keep working on it until it is clear to you. Now, remember no repeats. So once an object is created, it cannot be repeated.

(Audience laughter)

Just let it happen. You can do so sound effects if you want... like "ho ho!"

(Audience laughter)

> (The group silently creates different objects and passes them to their left as instructed)

Okay, great. You need to use what she has given you first.

(Audience member with Scottish dialect makes a bagpipe: "Oh, bloody hell, I can't play this thing!")

Okay, we have a few actors in the group today.

(Audience member: "I need to put this into your mouth... louder... louder!")

(Audience applauds)
That is a perfect example of using the object as an extension of something else.
(Audience laughter)
(Audience member creates a vibrator then groans in ecstasy)
I bet none of you thought we would see that one.
(Audience laughter)

44

How Bouncing a Ball Can Become Flying a Kite

Acting it out

OUR CIRCLE EXERCISE was a warm up and a nice evolution of receiving something using it and taking it to another level. Now one more time around with a bouncing ball.
   (Audience member: "Where's the ball?")
   Oh? I forgot to tell you. You are going to create the ball.
   (Audience laughter)
   The ball that we create is just the starting point. Now what I want you to do is create a ball. Not too big. Not too small. Something the size of a basket ball and I want you to start by bouncing on the floor. Just like you would a basketball. Like this.
   (Catalano demonstrates)
   Okay, now you try it.
   Just bounce the ball and then pass it back to me. Okay, so now I have just caught a bouncing ball from her – now I want to have you think about accepting what you get… sometimes when you get something in an improvisation, you just don't change it on the spot. Okay, now we have established a bouncing ball as our starting point but

remember what we talked about. The bouncing ball is just the starting point – then the physical "bouncing" can evolve into something else quite different. The hard part here is for you to let it evolve on its own and not try to force something on it. Just let it evolve on its own and see where it leads you.

We are starting today with a bouncing ball but this could be a more complex idea that starts out one way and then becomes something else. An improvisational scene works the same way – you can place your characters into one idea and on its own evolves into something totally different.

(Catalano passes the ball to the Audience member)

One more time if you don't mind.

(Audience member bounces the ball again and passes it back to him)

Okay, she passes me a bouncing ball. I am just using this physicality of bouncing a ball, but slowly it starts to change.

(Catalano mimes bouncing a ball)

Now as we speak, this ball (or physicality) is taking on a life of its own and slowly becoming something else. What will it become? I'm not sure.

(Catalano's movements start to change)

It's clearly becoming something else… but I am not sure what it is… because I'm talking to all of you and I can't do two things at one time. It's okay to not know what it's going to be… it's okay to not "think" too much about this. You're just allowing it to happen and let it become something else. As it changes my physicality begins to evolve.

(Catalano's movement change slowly)

I truly have no control over this other than I am using the energy of the physicality to take me to another physicality.

(Slowly Catalano's movements change from bouncing a ball to flying a kite.)

I had no idea that I would be flying a kite today and now we have something entirely different.

(He stops moving.)

So what happened? I started out bouncing a ball and it evolved on its own into flying a kit. So my part within the creative process with this simple example was to allow it to happen on its own and then to "select" what it became as it evolved. I could have let it go longer and it might have evolved into something else. This is the process you must undertake when you utilize improvisation to expand your characters and storyline of your novels. It will also assist you with the adaptation process in converting your novels into screenplays or plays for the theatre.

Now, I would like you all to pair up and try this exercise on your own. You don't have to start with a bouncing ball. You can pick any physical activity. Once you have established that activity then pass it on to your partner. Don't pass it on until you both know what it is. If the person receiving doesn't know send it back.

> (Approximately five minutes passes as audience performs both parts of the exercise.)

Okay, so now we know how a bouncing ball can become flying a kit. You can do the same process of discovery using words along with your actions. Shall we give it a try?

How much time do we have left?

(Staff member indicates a short amount of time.)

We will do a shortened version with words because we are almost out of time for today.

I want you all to stay in your groupings of two. Identify who is "A" and who is "B."

Good. Now I want the "A" people to come up with a word. Don't say it.

Does everyone have one? Good. Now start your improvisation with that one word just like you did with the bouncing ball. Just say the word and "B" just respond with a word. Keep going until you have evolved into talking in sentences.

Okay, go!

(Approximately three minutes pass.)

Okay, please take a seat.

How many people here within this short period of time started to develop characters and a situation – "Who" and "What."
(Several audience members raise their hands)
What kind of relationships did you discover?
(Audience members raise their hands)
(Audience member: "Husband and Wife.")
Okay.
(Audience member: "Shoe salesman and customer."
All right!
(Audience member: "Boyfriend and girlfriend breaking up.")
Ouch!
All right, in that instance we have both characters and situation.
Great.

Our time is almost up for today. We have to give up this conference room to the next program. I want you all to know if there any questions about any of the concepts that we have discussed today, that I am available just outside

45

ACTING IT OUT

USING IMPROVISATION CAN help writers to think out the box. When we get up on our feet, it forces us to use all of our senses and try ideas that we might otherwise reject if we sat in front of our laptops thinking about it.

This is an important point. As writers we have the tendency to think too much. So Acting it out is way to cut the thinking or intellectual process off. It allows our other creative sources to kick and take us to places we might no otherwise go. When we intellectualize we edit and when we edit we stop or slow down the creative process.

When we act out we find that every story has a who, what when and where automatically. On our feet we experience it in the same way the audience experiences it. If we let our creative juices flow, our role then becomes one of a selective process. Where we can select from those ideas or elements we discover. Getting up on our feet and acting it out makes us look at our ideas in many new ways. Which take me to my next point – that is listening.

We talked about listening today and through listening we should find a creative means of acceptance. We discussed that we have to accept those elements introduced within an improvisation. Remember our example of the elevator. One actor says can you press the 14th floor and the other rejects it and says they are on a bus stop. We instead have to look at the creative process as we act it out as one where we accept every element with a "Yes" and then we using our own creativity use an "and" and add something to it. In this manner, we can discover elements of our original idea that we may never have thought about. This is a simple process that allows us to go on a journey and not always know where it will lead.

It's also important to make interesting choices and avoid being literal. Remember our example of the improvisation about the apple. The original word was "apple" and then the entire scene was about the apple. Instead we talked about raising the stakes and making the apple represent something quite different. In this case, the apple would just be the starting point. We can raise the stakes through intensifying our character's desires or motivations to do what they do and of course provide internal or external obstacles to prevent them from achieving what they want. Audiences like a happy ending where everything works out – but they also want to work for it. We don't want to make it easy, funny and without any tension. Even comedy has tension. If we all just agree to agree we really don't have drama.

Now we have come full circle. Remember that improvisation is a tool for writers to use to create more interesting stories and characters. This means that not everything you discover will work. Improvisation just takes you there and presents you with a choice. You have to select those elements that work for your story and reject those that do not. That is the essence of the creative process.

Think of Thomas Edison and his greatest achievement of perfecting a light bulb.

> Edison: "Negative results are just what I want. They're just as valuable to me as positive results. I can never find the thing that does the job best until I find the ones that don't."

Using improvisation and acting out your ideas is your method of experimentation.

I want to thank you all for being such a great group today! Give yourselves a hand! Thank you again for attending ACTING IT OUT as part of the 25th Annual Writer's Conference.

(Audience applause)

WRITING GREAT DIALOGUE

SAN DIEGO STATE UNIVERSITY
25th Annual Writers Conference

HOW TO ADAPT YOUR NOVEL INTO A SCREENPLAY

BOOK 7

Frank Catalano

46

WRITING GREAT DIALOGUE

Writing Great Dialogue

THE PURPOSE OF today's seminar is writing great dialogue that can be writing dialogue within the context of a novel, play or a screenplay. Now most of you are fiction writers here today. If you take what you have written and develop your material into a screenplay, you would have to take your fictional work, which may be between 300 – 400 pages and have to reduce it down to a screenplay of 120 pages.

Your task would be to take your story, characters and description and fit them into an entirely new format designed for a new media. I want to say up front that I'm not counting pages. I don't do that. So if your screenplay turns out to be 130 pages that's fine with me. There are no hard fast rules of engagement here, where you fall through a trap door in the floor into a pool of alligators if your screenplay is longer than 120 pages.

(Audience laughter)

What I am saying is that if you write your screenplay in the appropriate format and it is for a full-length motion picture, it is going to come out around 120 pages. An excellent format book for appropriate screenplay format is **The Complete Guide to Standard Script Formats, Part 1** by Judith H. Haag and Hillis R. Cole.

If you adapt your 400-page novel into a screenplay and it is 200 pages, it is too long for the intended medium of a motion picture. It might work as a mini series or limited series. A mini series can fun from three to four and half hours. A limited series would be more likely one-hour episodes with a smaller number to completion of each season. Let's say eight to ten. It is not the same as a mini series that are really extended movies for television running on the average three to four hours in length.

The target page number for motion picture screenplay is approximately 120 pages, which will translate into a roughly two-hour film. Okay, so who makes up these rules? Why does the motion picture format have to be that length?

If it is coming through the door as a "spec" script, it will be looked at differently than a project, which is studio, developed or brought in by a well-established producer or writer.

Now even though you are writing a script that originates from a novel that you authored, it will still be considered a spec script. When it is read, and it will be read or covered, the reader will want to access your ability to convey characters and story for the film medium. We discussed this earlier this week that fictional writing is quite different than cinematic storytelling. In short, they will want to be able to connect to your story and characters within what will be a two-hour presentational framework. It is generally accepted that the running time of the average motion picture should be approximately one hundred-twenty minutes. As a screenwriter, you must decide what elements of your novel to include and make decisions the will enable you to you're your story in that amount of time. That's the creative reason, but there is also a business reason to craft your screenplay within 120 pages.

47

PRODUCTION DISTRIBUTION EXHIBITION

Writing Great Dialogue

THE CREATIVE PROCESS, which takes a motion picture from its inception, to production to distribution to finally showing at your local movie theatre, can be divided into three categories.

Production:
This is the development and implementation of the creative idea that includes the writing, the production, actors, directors, designers and producers, which participate in the making of the movie. Once the movie is completed and studio management approves the final cut of the negative, the film is locked. They used to call it "in the can." But that's not really true anymore because most if not all films are digital. The can no longer exists... it's now a digital file. But the process remains the same. Once the final cut of the film is approved it is ready for distribution.

Distribution:
This is the marketing and "distribution" of the film to individual outlets such as movie theatres. If the film were intended for other outlets

such as streaming or DVD, this would be the same process. This process includes the marketing, posters, and advertisements, talent interviews that promote and distribute the final film to the public. Years ago it also would include the physical creation of "prints" of the film on celluloid to be distributed to movie theatres around the world. Once the film is delivered and the marketing is in place, the process of exhibition takes place.

Exhibition:
This is true to the meaning of the word. It is the physical playing or showing of the final film (print) to the public. In short, it's your local multiplex or cinema. It is the brick and mortar movie theatre, the seats, the popcorn, the candy, and the tickets. All that sort of thing. The showing of the film to the public.

Today, Production and distribution are a separate process from exhibition. During the golden age of cinema, the five major studios (Warner Brothers, 20th Century Fox, MGM, Universal and Paramount) owned all three - production, distribution and exhibition. This was called the Studio System and everyone who worked on a movie during the 1930's through the early 1950's worked as a contracted employee. That meant that the studio owned 100% of whatever they produced and kept all of the profits. They even owned the physical brick and motor theatres that their films were shown in. So, what was produced and shown was totally in the hands of the studio bosses in Los Angeles and corporate heads in New York City.

In 1948, that all changed when the Supreme Court ruled that this practice of 100% ownership was a monopoly and after that the studio system was dead. The five major studios were forced to sell off the exhibition part of the business. They retained production and distribution but had to sell off all of their theatres. Today, when movies are produced, they are not guaranteed an endless run at a company owned movie theatre. If they don't attract and audience, they are pulled from the theatre and replaced with another film.

What does all this have to do with taking you novel and creating a screenplay? Motion picture exhibitors (owners of multiplexes) don't like movies that are too long. Why?

They want to be able to get as many showings in a given exhibition space as possible. So if there is a question of tradition that a screenplay has to be approximately 120 pages, there is also the practical matter that modern films cannot be too long. This is a general statement and you can probably site lots of successful exceptions such *as Saving Private Ryan (1998 – 170 minutes), Lord of the Rings (2001 – 178 minutes) King Kong (2005 – 187 minutes, Pearl Harbor (2001 – 183 minutes) and Gone Girl (2014 – 149 minutes –* but the vast majority of features run approximately 120 minutes. I read a recent article in Business Insider that actually is trending movie run times as getting longer – from a 2010 average of 113 minutes to an average run time of 130 minutes. However, what's driving this data are the larger than life studio owned blockbuster films like *Transformers – Age of Extinction (165 minutes), The Amazing Spiderman II* (142 minutes) and *Dawn of the Planet of the Apes* (130 minutes). Your screenplay will not enter the production process as a studio owned project. It will come in as a spec script with perhaps a star or director attached. It you want it to have a chance; it is best to keep it within the two hour 120 page format.

By the way, if you are adapting your book into a teleplay to be released as a movie for network television – the usual run time is 120 minutes including commercial breaks. The actual runtime without the commercials is approximately 88 minutes. So what you include in your teleplay has to fit within that specific runtime.

So now you have got to look at your novel and make decisions about how to create the same quality of story and character within the shorter format. You may have multiple story lines, sub plots and a wide variety of characters. How do you fit this all into such a specific and limited timeframe?

It is these varied elements of character and story that make your novel complex and interesting. It is the very reason that people want to read it. So now you take what you have done and squeeze into a much smaller creative box or you can select specific elements out of the whole. In either case, you will have to make choices about what you are going to use and what you are going to omit. The truth is that many excellent multifaceted novels can actually make more than one movie. I am not talking about spinning off a concept. I am talking about the actual novel being the source for more than one movie. I'm thinking of Michael Crichton's novels *Jurassic Park (1990)* and *The Lost World (1995)* were the source material for *Jurassic Park (1993)*, *The Lost World – Jurassic Park (1997)*, *Jurassic Park III (2001)* and *Jurassic World (2015)*. The original novels were two encompassing for just one film, so the material as an idea of origination or actual story and character was developed into three motion pictures.

So you have to think about what elements of your work you will want to incorporate into the screenplay version. You will want to select those elements of your character and story that will be best suited to translate into the visual medium of film. But remember, you can't take it all with you. You will have to fight the urge of trying to squeeze it all in. Of course, there may be someone who sees the film and says, "I read the book and the book is much better than the film."

(Audience laughter)

The book is better? Well maybe it is… and maybe it isn't. The truth is that the book and the movie are two very different things. Your challenge is to keep as much of the intricacy and texture of your book within the new visual medium of film. Think as if you were a painter like Michelangelo and you had to paint the Sistine Chapel with only four colors of paint.

(Audience laughter)

You would have to think about which four colors you would retain to convey your original idea. Yes?

(Audience members nod in agreement)

48

DESCRIPTION ACTION DIALOGUE

Now in a screenplay, as we have talked about in some of my seminars this weekend, you have three elements of expression – Description, Action and Dialogue. Let me quickly review this:

Description:
This where you briefly describe the setting or character in a screenplay by giving the reader just enough information to get an idea of what is going on. What it is not is a long description that you might include in a novel. Where then does the detail come into play? Once the screenplay goes into the production phase, actors, directors and designers will fill in the blanks that your description simply indicates.

Action:
Briefly tells the reader what physically is happening with the characters and setting. Be specific enough that a person reading the script will know what's going on but not so detailed as to be clinical. "He lifted up his left arm slowly and easily touched his nose with his index finger and thumb." Just keep it simple "He effortlessly touched his nose with his left hand."

Dialogue:
On it's face value it is what your characters say. However, how they say it and what they don't say is also revealing.

Think of your screenplay as a blueprint for a more expanded action whereas your novel might elaborate on these elements in much fuller detail. In your books you may have used metaphors to create vivid descriptions of characters and setting. In a screenplay, you just lay it out briefly but creatively. You know you're doing it right when you can take two pages of description, action and dialogue from your book and fit it into three lines in your screenplay.

I want you know that you can't just copy and paste large swaths of text from your novel and paste them into your screenplay. It is a totally different mode of expression. If you think of your book, you visualize large blocks of text. If you visualize your screenplay, visualize large blocks of white space. With all of this said, you just can't cut the guts out of your book – you have to keep the spirit of it – but you just have to do it in a much smaller space and setting. You have to constantly strive to find the economy of words. You also have to let go. What do I mean by let go? Many screenwriters want to squeeze in every bit of detail because they visualize a particular character or scene in a certain way. I think you have to make choices that reflect the spirit of your novel but then let go. Leave space for the director, the actors and designers to add their talents to your work. Make your screenplay a truly collaborative work.

Earlier this week, we did an exercise where I asked the all of the novelists in the room to take a page of their book and boil it down to just three lines of text for a screenplay. There was a lot of groaning to be sure.

(Audience laughter)

But in the end, most of them got pretty close. If you try hard enough you can find the right words that are not pedestrian that can capture the essence and the poetry that you have discovered in your fictional work. You achieve the terseness of the screenwriting form without losing the underlying soul of your work. It's like walking on a tightrope.

Now let's talk about dialogue.

49

WHAT DOES DIALOGUE DO?

Writing Great Dialogue

WHAT DOES DIALOGUE do?

> (Audience members raise their hands)

Yes?

> (Audience members call out)

It dramatizes the character.

It communicates ideas to the audience and other characters.

It can show us how the character expresses their inner hopes and dreams.

It can tell us something about the character... meaning dialect, educational level, attitude or emotional state.

We can also learn about "back story" through expositional dialogue.

Any others?

Move the story forward.

Create dramatic tension.

Great. All very good. But I have a question for all of you. Can "action" do any of the same things that you have indicated?

Yes, action can do all of these things as well.

So one of the first things I will say about writing great dialogue is you don't always have to speak. Remember film is visual. If you can show it without saying it that is something I would like you to consider. Why? Because we want the dialogue we *do* write, to be dynamic and forceful. We want to use our words sparingly to achieve the greatest impact.

Let's do a short example.

(Catalano approaches an audience member)

Ask me how I am? Okay?

(Audience member: "Okay... how are you?")

(Catalano folds his arms tightly and frowns)

I'm fine.

(Audience laughter)

What do you think? Am I really fine?

(Audience member: "No.")

How do you know that?

(Audience member: "By your action. You frowned and had your arms folded tightly.")

Okay, so my action said something about my character without having the character actually speak it?

(Audience member: "Right.")

So, here it is. Your first consideration in Writing Great Dialogue is to speak only when you actually have to. If you can accomplish what you want to do with action, then do it. Look at your characters in your book and try to determine if they can communicate to an audience through action instead of dialogue. You ever hear that adage – "Don't tell me... show me?" You want to enable the reader of your screenplay to experience your story through actions, thoughts, senses, and feelings rather than through your written exposition and description. So you see, we *are* talking about dialogue or at least functionally to achieve what dialogue can do within a story.

Let's think about what you can do with a simple action.

There is a long section of description of a husband who comes home every night from work, kicks off his shoes and takes off his socks and leaves them scattered on the floor. This action is followed by a one page monologue by his wife who details to the reader that he does this every night and that they will remain there on the floor unless she picks them up and how now (at this moment) she is not going to take it any more. It ends on this night. She will never pick up his socks again.

So, how can we replace the entire monologue with one line of action?

The husband walks into the house, takes his shoes and socks off and leaves them scattered on the floor. His wife, sighs deeply, picks them up (he smiles) then throws them into the garbage pale, picks up a suitcase and walks out the front door.

This short sequence of action conveys the same information to the audience without the long monologue. It says something about the two characters as well as communicates a situation to an audience. Not everything needs to be spoken.

Do you remember those old movies in the thirties… with their terse dialogue?

(Catalano with English dialect)

Tea?

Yes.

Sugar?

Thank you.

Delightful.

Hot?

Yes, very…

They would create scenes with a minimum of dialogue and just using the physicality and action to create the characters and situation.

Language in the traditional sense that we might think of when writing literature will have to be transposed into the visual medium of film. Film is visual. If you can tell (show) your story visually rather than tell it – that is the better choice. Screenplays show us… novels tell us… and as we have spoken about this weekend… our world is visual. Television and the Internet have made us a visual society – so anytime you can visualize an intellectual idea or an emotion – do it.

Now what about dialogue itself?

Dialogue is the talking.

It can also be talking accompanied by action. We saw this in our small example of this nice person asking me if I was fine. We had a short dialogue accompanied by a specific physical action.

And that physical action – changed the meaning of the scene entirely.

The actual words were

How are you?

I am fine.

On its face value, I am fine. But when the folded arms and frown were added to my response, it revealed that I was actually the opposite of fine. Let's do it again.

Ask me how I am.

(Audience member: "How are you?")

(Catalano frowns and folds his arms)

I am fine.

So we can see that my actions change the meaning. So you can combine action with dialogue and have it influence its meaning.

Now the dialogue.

How can you use dialogue to further all of your characters development within the story? What you write about them when you first introduce them. That might include their age range, physical stature and a unique characteristic about them or the way they interact in their universe. Now remember, you won't be able to write long paragraphs about your character in your screenplay – so we have to learn about them in three ways.

1. What do your characters say about themselves? Is what they say the truth or are they lying?
2. What do other characters say about your characters? Is it the truth or are they lying?
3. What do your characters say to other characters in your story that reveals who they are and what their motivation is within their universe?

So, how can we accomplish this? I want you to think about what I will call the three P's

Professional: What a characters does for a living.

Personal: What are your characters relationships in the universe?

Private: Something secret that only your character knows about themselves.

Now think about this at our conference this weekend. When you meet people for the first time, you see their nametags and all that but at some point in the conversation don't you finally ask them what they do?

(Catalano in deep voice)

Hello I'm Mr. Smith. Hello Mr. Smith, I'm Mr. Jones... **what do you do?**

(Audience laughter)

Thank you... I bet you didn't know I did all these character voices.

(Audience laughter)

So in this brief introduction we learn what they do or in the case of this conference, everyone wants to know what genre you are in.

Right?

(Audience laughter?)

You could also add action to the scene by having one of the characters be a close talker – you know those types of people who invade your personal space.

(Audience laughter)

(Catalano in a deep voice again)

Hello I'm Mr. Smith. Hello Mr. Smith, I'm Mr. Jones... **what do you do?**

Smith moves in too close and replies – "I write erotic thrillers."

Jones steps back: "I see…"

(Audience laughter)

This helps frame your character in a professional way. Doctor, lawyer or police officer, everyone wants to know what we do. They also want to know (I don't know why), what our personal situation is.

They want to know if we are married or attached in any way, widowed, divorced, engaged, single, gay, straight… you don't have to come right out and say it.

Hello, I'm Mr. Smith, I'm a gay widower who has recently broken up with his fiancé and is now single.

(Audience laughter)

No but use dialogue to reveal little things about your character's personal situation. Their personal situation will often influence how they react to the universe they live in. The last one I mentioned today is private.

We all have secrets that no one else knows about ourselves. So if it's a secret we don't talk about it right? No, your characters secrets can be revealed (if even a glimpse of them) through what they say or don't say. Your character could be exalted as a hero but secretly be a coward who is afraid of his or her own shadow. You can use dialogue to create the tension between these two qualities. I am thinking about a novel I read a long time ago called *The Red Badge of Courage* that is a war novel by American author Stephen Crane (1871–1900). The main character is a coward that is tormented because he fled the battlefield – but then is thought of as a hero when his regiment once again faces the enemy; the soldier acts as standard-bearer and hero. This secret was one that no one else knew but the soldier – but it influenced his actions within the story of the book.

So ask yourself, do your main characters hold any secrets or private moments within their universe? Aristotle in his **Poetics** discusses the concept of hamartia or fatal flaw leading to the downfall of a tragic hero or heroine. Your character's private element as revealed by his dialogue can lead to his/her tragic downfall. Think of William Shakespeare's Macbeth when he says:

> "*I have no spur To prick the sides of my intent,*
> *but only Vaulting ambition,*
> *which o'erleaps itself,*
> *And falls on th'other. . . .*"

His private demon is his ambition. And it is his ambition that pushes Macbeth to murder the king and eventually bring him to his own downfall.

I call these Professional, Personal and Private the three "P's" that you can reveal using spoken dialogue and action. Let's go back to the beginning – the four colors. So you are reducing what you have in your novel to fit into your screenplay but you are also adding new dimensions. Selecting elements of your characters to highlight and underscore through spoken words and action within their universe.

A character's universe is the world they live within. This could include the time period, the geography, the time of year, the time of day, the cultural framework as well as the character's place within that universe.

If your character lives in Victorian England are they rich or poor? If they are rich, they would talk and have a certain physicality – if they were poor it would be another. The Victorian period as a whole would be more formal than let's say the 1960's in the way people spoke to one another. It doesn't have to be a time period change – it can be contemporary.

I remember one episode of a television show I was working on when they asked me to write a scene for two doctors talking while they were doing a routine surgery on a patient. At first I thought about writing a highly technical scene and have them talk within a framework of medical terms. But then, I thought that more than likely they would talk about other things like sports, the stock market what they did over the weekend and that dialogue would be peppered with medical terms. I called the hospital for a consult and I was correct. So their universe (the two surgeons) even though they were performing surgery was much more informal than one might think. Dialogue can also be influence by plot.

What's the situation? Is it a blind date, a funeral a job interview? Just think of the times you might have gone on a job interview or important meeting. Did you have a specific kind of physicality and way you spoke? Did you use different kinds of words? Some analysts and sales consultants teach their sales personal to "mimic" their prospect.

Essentially, after speaking for a few moments – very slowly – the sales person begins to mimic the physical state, vocal quality and way of speaking of someone they want to sell to. I guess the idea is that people like to buy things from other people that are just like them. The same can be said of creating "opposites" by creating a physical state, dialogue that is direct opposition to the character they are speaking.

So, dialogue can be your way to further your story and develop your character in your screenplay.

How much time do we have left?

(Administrator: "Five minutes.")

50

OTHER QUALITIES OF DIALOGUE

Writing Great Dialogue

OKAY. I WANT you to think about how your characters sound when they speak. Now you may think, doesn't that depend upon the actor saying those lines? Yes and no. I want you to create an auditory signature in your brain that sets up in your mind and eventually your reader's mind how your character dispenses the dialogue they speak.

Do any of you remember the movie *And Justice for All* (1979) with Al Pacino?

(Almost all of the audience members raise their hands)

If you haven't seen it, you should check it out.

Remember that famous scene where Al Pacino says:

"You're out of order! You're out of order! The whole trial is out of order! They're out of order! That man, that sick, crazy, depraved man, raped and beat that woman there, and he'd like to do it again! He *told* me so! It's just a show! It's a show! It's "Let's Make A Deal"!

"Let's Make A Deal"! Hey Frank, you wanna "Make A Deal"? I got an insane judge who likes to beat the shit out of women! Whaddya wanna gimme Frank, 3 weeks probation?"

or when Don Corleone as the *Godfather (1972)* speaks in his graveled voice:

(Catalano does Godfather voice)

"I'm gonna make him an offer he can't refuse."

(Audience laughter)

Thank you. I will be doing film impressions today at 4:00 PM in the Lido Room!

(Audience laughter)

There really isn't a Lido Room is there? I didn't think so.

Each of these characters has their own vocal quality and sound that makes them unique.

This next point is a bit tricky. But I start it with a question. When your character speaks, do they talk in a presentational manner – in elevated tones like they are are on stage?

Some characters relish every word they speak as it they were spun of gold. I'm thinking of Sherlock Holmes and more specifically Basil Rathbone's creation of the character.

"It seemed to me that a careful examination of the room and the lawn might possibly reveal some traces of this mysterious individual. You know my methods, Watson. There was not one of them which I did not apply to the inquiry. And it ended by my discovering traces, but very different ones from those which I had expected."

This is a *presentational* type of quality. If this is a quality your character possesses – illustrate it with presentational dialogue. These types of characters are always presenting themselves to the world. They are talking to another character but they are also at the same time talking to everyone else. The other type of character dialogue is *representational* where the spoken words are much more intimate and personal.

When a representational type of speaker talks to another character it is much more intimate and you get a sense of who they are and where they come from. They are not "on" when they speak – they speak and convey emotions and intellectual ideas directly with no concern of their presentation.

What about dialect? When you convey dialect it's probably best to write it actually as you want it spoken. There may be other opinions about this but from my perspective I would like to have the utmost control over how my character speaks. Now if you write it this way and they cast an actor who doesn't want or can't do that way, they will change it. Think about Rhett Butler in *Gone with the Wind (1939)* – Clark Gable just spoke the way he normally did. Now he didn't do a southern dialect by made up for it with physicality, action and a larger than life personality. One other thing about dialect, if you write it phonetically make sure it is understandable on the page when its read. You don't want your reader dwelling upon a phrase because they don't know what it means.

I know I'm almost out of time – but I also wanted to mention dialogue rhythm. Does your character speak in a certain rhythm or repeat phrases? Do they use malapropisms when trying to identify an idea or person?

I'm thinking of films like *Gone with the Wind* when Scarlett says:

As God is my witness,
as God is my witness they're not going to lick me.
I'm going to live through this and when it's all over,

I'll never be hungry again.
No, nor any of my folk.
If I have to lie, steal, cheat or kill.
As God is my witness, I'll never be hungry again.

Or the motion *picture Goodfellas (1990)*

(Catalano does an imitation of Joe Pesci)

What do you mean, you mean the way I talk?
What? You mean, let me understand this cause, ya' know maybe it's me,
I'm funny how, I mean funny like I'm a clown,
I amuse you? I make you laugh?
I'm here to amuse you?
What do you mean funny, funny how? How am I funny?

(Audience applause)

I took out the dirty words... but I just wanted to give you an idea of rhythm.

Also create a sound for your character – just as a violin and a tuba (which both play music) might sound. Each instrument achieves that differently. Every character's voice has a certain sound and shape.

We are out of time.

In conclusion... and I know you all want to do a really great job in converting your novel to a screenplay. If you undertake this just write from the heart. Forget about everything we talked about today.

(Audience laughter)

Don't worry about the page count... just write from the heart. Don't worry about labels like EXTERIOR, INTERIOR, FADE OUT, and FADE IN – just write it! Visualize your novel from the heart and once you get it all down on paper – you can edit it to make it all fit. What a lot of writers to is edit as they write – trying to get it all done on the first draft. What happens? They never get done because they are always fixing one thing or another. It will never get completed and sit in your drawer like a jacked up Chevy in the garage doomed to incompletion.

Just write it! Thank you very much if there are any questions I am available outside in the hotel lobby.

(Audience applause)

Thank you and have a great rest of the day!

www.ingramcontent.com/pod-product-compliance
Lightning Source LLC
Chambersburg PA
CBHW050552170426
43201CB00011B/1670